A Guide to Mark

FAITH AND UNDERSTANDING

Many people, both Christians and others, have very good and legitimate questions about the Christian faith. This series is designed to address some of those contemporary questions. The series features modest-length books designed for non-specialist readers—average "people in the pews" rather than theological students or seminary graduates. Each book gives the reader the basics of the subject matter, and a bit beyond the basics. The authors seek to open doors for readers to learn more about Christian faith and life—and why it matters in contemporary society.

Series Editors:
Frank W. Hughes
Raymond F. Collins
Sheila E. McGinn

A Guide to Mark

Frank W. Hughes

CASCADE *Books* • Eugene, Oregon

A GUIDE TO MARK

Copyright © 2025 Frank W. Hughes. All rights reserved. Except for brief quotations in critical publications or reviews, no part of this book may be reproduced in any manner without prior written permission from the publisher. Write: Permissions, Wipf and Stock Publishers, 199 W. 8th Ave., Suite 3, Eugene, OR 97401.

Cascade Books
An Imprint of Wipf and Stock Publishers
199 W. 8th Ave., Suite 3
Eugene, OR 97401

www.wipfandstock.com

PAPERBACK ISBN: 979-8-3852-1163-0
HARDCOVER ISBN: 979-8-3852-1164-7
EBOOK ISBN: 979-8-3852-1165-4

Cataloguing-in-Publication data:

Names: Hughes, Frank W. (Frank Witt), 1954, author.

Title: A guide to Mark / Frank W. Hughes.

Description: Eugene, OR: Cascade Books, 2025. | Includes bibliographical references and indexes.

Identifiers: ISBN 979-8-3852-1163-0 (paperback). | ISBN 979-8-3852-1164-7 (hardcover). | ISBN 979-8-3852-1165-4 (epub).

Subjects: LSCH: Bible. Mark—Criticism, interpretation, etc. | Bible. Mark—Commentaries.

Classification: BS2585.5 H79 2025 (print). | BS2585.5 (epub).

Unless otherwise noted, Scripture quotations are taken from the New Revised Standard Version Bible, copyright © 1989 National Council of the Churches of Christ in the United States of America. Used by permission. All rights reserved worldwide.

Contents

Preface and Acknowledgments | vii

1. Why and How to Study the Gospels | 1
2. Introducing the Gospel according to Mark | 14
   Mark 1:1–15
3. Jesus's Ministry in Galilee | 24
   Mark 1:16—3:6
4. Further Ministry in Galilee | 37
   Mark 3:7—4:34
5. Miracles, Rejection, and Murder | 46
   Mark 4:35—6:56
6. Defilement and More Miracle Stories | 59
   Mark 7:1—8:26
7. Predictions of Suffering, Death, and Resurrection | 69
   Mark 8:27—10:52
8. Jesus in Jerusalem | 86
   Mark 11:1—13:37
9. The Passion of Jesus | 102
   Mark 14:1—15:47
10. The Resurrection | 114
    Mark 16:1–8 [9–20]
11. Reflections on Mark as a Whole | 118

Bibliography | 131
Index of Scripture and Other Ancient Literature | 141
Index of Authors | 149

Preface and Acknowledgments

ST. JEROME, THE FAMOUS biblical translator, wrote, "Ignorance of Scripture is ignorance of Christ."[1] Another early Christian writer, St. Gregory the Great, wrote, "Scripture is like a river again, broad and deep, shallow enough here for the lamb to go wading, but deep enough there for the elephant to swim."[2] Those quotations from two of the most dedicated scholars of the Bible who ever lived are challenging. The first quotation makes it clear that the Scriptures are vitally important to us as Christians. We don't want to be ignorant of Christ. Yet the beauty and complexity of the large tapestry of the texts of the Bible are often intimidating. There is so much to read, so much to try to understand, so much to learn! Scripture is really important, and Scripture is also clearly complicated, even just reading the Bible in English translation, to say nothing of reading it in its original languages.

Yet, when we begin to read Holy Scripture, we can always begin somewhere. To reiterate what St. Gregory said: a baby can drink from it without drowning, and theologians can swim in it without ever standing up and touching bottom. To extend St. Gregory's analogy, this book is intended for people who would prefer the shallow end of the swimming pool of Scripture, at least for a time. You do not have to dive into the deep end to get into the water. Yet after you do enter the pool at the shallow end, it would be good to venture into the other parts of the pool, because you probably will want to know what the pool as a whole is like. In the New Testament, you can start with any of the Gospels, or any of the Letters. Mark is a very

---

1. This statement is found in Jerome's *Commentary on Isaiah*, in *Patrologia Latina* 24.17 (my translation).

2. St. Gregory the Great, *Moralia*, 4, found in *Patrologia Latina* 75.515. The English translation of this quotation is found at https://faculty.georgetown.edu/jod/texts/moralia1.html.

good place to start because it is generally believed to be the major source of Matthew and Luke. It may have been a source for John as well.

For a number of reasons, the Gospel According to Mark continues to be my favorite gospel. I can never read the Gospel according to Mark without a flood of memories of scholarship and scholars I have known. The first course I took in seminary in 1976 was a course with that very title, taught by a brash thirty-four-year-old scholar named Richard I. Pervo, who was starting his second year of teaching at Seabury-Western Theological Seminary. Later that year I came to know Wolfgang M. W. Roth, a distinguished scholar of the Hebrew Bible at Garrett-Evangelical Theological Seminary. In 1988 appeared Roth's provocative book on Mark; *Hebrew Gospel: Cracking the Code of Mark* argued that the Gospel of Mark was an *imitatio* of the Elijah/Elisha cycle of stories from the Hebrew Bible. In 1984 Vernon K. Robbins published a magisterial book on Mark, *Jesus the Teacher*, which was his earliest book on sociorhetorical criticism of the New Testament. Elizabeth Struthers Malbon's several books on Mark have brought literary criticism into the international discussion of Mark, first examining how the spatial setting of Mark, namely Galilee and Jerusalem, was a major factor in the shaping of Mark. More recently she has written on personification and characterization in Mark. I cannot fail to mention the excellent older commentaries by Henry Barclay Swete and Vincent Taylor and the fine recent commentaries by Pheme Perkins, C. Clifton Black, Darrell Bock, M. Eugene Boring, and Mary Ann Beavis among several others, and especially the magisterial commentary by Adela Yarbro Collins. More recently appeared the comprehensive and important monograph by David E. Garland, *A Theology of Mark's Gospel*.

This book is called *A Guide to Mark*, and by this title I mean a book that an interested person can use to help understand the Gospel of Mark. I hope that readers will discern the structure and content of Mark, and especially, what makes the Gospel According to Mark distinctive among the four Gospels of the New Testament. The most important feature of Mark is its overall message—in other words, what the author of Mark was trying to say to his or her readers. I am always asking myself these questions: What techniques and forms of persuasion were going on in the text of Mark, and what was the message worth persuading others to accept? So, broadly speaking, I am interested in the rhetoric of the Gospel of Mark. I hope you will understand both my asking these questions and my answers to the questions that I pose. My questions and answers, of course, are not

Preface and Acknowledgments

meant to preclude your consideration of your own questions and answers as you read and study an English translation of Mark.

I take this opportunity to thank other friends who have helped me in numerous ways, including reading the manuscript of this book. These friends include Professor Raymond F. Collins, the coeditor of this series, as well as two of my former parishioners, Myra Smith and Gayland Rushing of Trinity Episcopal Church in Longview, Texas, where I was privileged to serve as interim rector from 2017 to 2019, and where I did happily teach through the Gospel According to Mark. Another reader was my sister Cilla Hughes Trenado, who has helped me in ways far too numerous to list. Yet another reader was the Rev. Andrew Christiansen of St. Michael and All Angels Episcopal Church in Lake Charles, Louisiana. I am pleased to thank my parishioners at the Episcopal Church of the Redeemer in Ruston, Louisiana, as well as two other good friends who have enabled me to lecture through Mark in their parishes: the Rev. Michael Cannon of St. Paul's Episcopal Church in Shreveport, and the Rev. Don Smith of Grace Episcopal Church in Monroe. All these good people have helped me with their comments and questions, and none of them are responsible for the remaining imperfections in this book.

Some brief Scripture quotations are from the New Revised Standard Version Bible, copyright © 1989 National Council of the Churches of Christ in the United States of America. These quotations are used by permission. Other Scripture quotations are my own translations.

Frank W. Hughes
Spearsville, Louisiana
June 2024

1

Why and How to Study the Gospels

As we explore how to study the Gospels in the New Testament, it would be good to be clear about why we want to do so. There are many reasons to study the New Testament Gospels. Jesus of Nazareth was the most famous person who lived in the ancient world and probably the most famous person who ever lived in the history of the world. Christians are followers of Jesus, and Christianity is the religion in the world practiced by more people than any other religion. So, assuming that Christianity is at least culturally important, it follows that we would want to know as much as possible about the person who founded Christianity. It is natural that we would want to know as much as possible about how this religion started, and what relationship there is between Jesus and Christianity. Even if we could know little about Jesus himself, what the Christian churches have taught and continue to teach about Jesus remains important to the history of world civilizations. For this reason, all the writings of early followers of Jesus, whenever and by whom they were written, are of importance in order for us to gain a good understanding of the Christian religion.

Of course, for Christians there is the added reason for study of the Gospels: we Christians would like to know what Jesus was like and what he taught and did so that we might be able, as best we can, to imitate his life and follow his commands. Christians believe that Jesus was God incarnate, God in human flesh, so naturally we are curious about what Jesus's earthly life was like. To move towards being in the best relationship with God, we Christians would like to learn, among other things, what Jesus taught his earliest followers, what he did when sick people were presented to him for healing, whether or not he predicted his suffering and death, and what he thought he was doing when he went to Jerusalem at the end of his natural life. As Christians, we pray in the name of Jesus and for the sake of Jesus. We do what we can do to extend the compassion and mercy of Jesus to other people. We are all fully aware of the summary of the law of God in Matt 22:38: "the greatest and first commandment" is to love God, and "a second one is like it, 'You shall love your neighbor as yourself.'" About these two commands from the Torah of Moses (Deut 6:5 and Lev 19:18 respectively) Jesus commented that the entire Torah and Prophets hang on them. So for Christians, as for Jews, it is a sacred obligation for us both to love God and to love our neighbors. We need to understand and obey both of those commandments.

Going Back to Jesus

Since Christians have a special set of reasons for studying the Gospels in the New Testament, because of their initiation and formation in and commitment to the Christian religion, it is natural and reasonable that Christians would want to know as much as possible about the founder of their religion, Jesus of Nazareth. By learning what Jesus did and taught his earliest followers to do, the knowledge gained by the study of the Gospels should inspire Christians today to be better followers of Christ so that they can teach and commend the Christian faith more effectively to others. Such knowledge might well make the church better than it is.

Since you are reading this book, I am assuming that you are at least moderately interested in Jesus of Nazareth and what we can know about him, and especially what we can learn about Jesus from reading and studying the Gospel According to Mark. Those of us who are Christians believe that the Bible is inspired. Our belief in the inspiration of Scripture means that we believe the Holy Spirit inspired the writer of the Gospel of Mark—however the material in Mark was compiled, composed, and edited. Thus, being a Christian—or not—or being a person interested in the Christian religion—or not—really does make a difference when a person sits down to read the Gospel According to Mark.

Whether or not you understand yourself to be a follower of Jesus, I strongly recommend that you now *read the Gospel According to Mark in its entirety*, in one or two sittings if you can. If you read Mark in two sittings,

I suggest that you read Mark 1:1—8:26 in the first sitting and Mark 8:27—16:8 in the second sitting. These two parts of Mark are just about equal in length, and an important event called the Confession of Peter begins in 8:27, and immediately following 8:27–30 there is Jesus's first prediction of his suffering and death. So, pausing your reading after 8:26 would give you a chance to think about (and perhaps to make some notes about) what you have read in the first half of Mark, before you go ahead with the second half. After you have read both halves of Mark, it would be helpful for you to try to identify the point of view that the writer of Mark had. Another good approach to reading Mark is for you to try to identify the questions that your reading of Mark raise in your mind both during and after your reading. After you have read the Gospel of Mark, most of what follows in this book should make sense to you.

The Historical Jesus

First of all, we are not the first readers to study the New Testament carefully. In order for you, my readers, to understand some of what my interests in Mark are, I need to go back into the history of scholarship briefly, to a time before twentieth-century form criticism, in which I was educated in the 1970s. I am going back to the classic Life-of-Jesus research chronicled by Albert Schweitzer in his brilliant classic *The Quest of the Historical Jesus*. Schweitzer drew on the controversial work of Hermann Samuel Reimarus from the late eighteenth century and went as far forward as Johannes Weiss in the early twentieth century.[1] To make a long and very involved story short, Reimarus ushered in a period in which the perspectives of the Enlightenment were applied to the study of the Gospels. Instead of asking questions that had to do with what Christian authorities had to say about Jesus, or what the Christian faith had traditionally said about the Bible, Reimarus and others used human reason in particular ways: they began to ask strongly historical questions about Jesus of Nazareth. Rather than writing about the "Christ of faith," the Life-of-Jesus researchers were interested in the "Jesus of history," namely, what one could learn and know about Jesus

---

1. Schweitzer, *Quest of the Historical Jesus*. After writing that "German theology will stand out as a great, a unique phenomenon in the mental and spiritual life of our time," Schweitzer referred to "the critical investigation of the life of Jesus" as "the greatest achievement of German theology" (3). Yet, as readers find out in the rest of Schweitzer's classic book, he was also deeply critical of the Life of Jesus movement, particularly when it did not use historical methods well.

of Nazareth, the actual first-century CE[2] person, using historical methods. A renowned German historian, Leopold von Ranke, taught students to use historical methods to determine "wie es eigentlich gewesen ist," which we can translate as "how it actually happened." The identification and analysis of sources, with a strong preference for earlier sources over later sources and, more especially, primary sources over secondary sources, became essential to biblical studies, especially as it developed in the nineteenth and twentieth centuries. To put it simply, in biblical scholarship we prefer to learn as much as we can about Jesus from the sources which are closest in time to Jesus. Christian theologians often found historical criticism of the Bible very congenial to their understanding of the Christian faith, for historically oriented biblical scholars affirmed that events like the exodus, the crucifixion and resurrection of Jesus, and the missionary efforts of the apostles really did happen. Abraham and Moses really existed, as did Jesus and Paul. These affirmations that biblical figures existed and that events in the Bible happened were (and are) necessary for Christian theology. It was necessary to argue that Paul, a real apostle, wrote several of the letters in the New Testament to real congregations in the first century CE. Further, we can trace quotations from Paul's Letters, including 1 Corinthians, Galatians, and Romans, along with quotations from the anonymous Letter to the Hebrews, in the First Letter of Clement, and so we can be certain that these Pauline letters and Hebrews were in existence and were believed by Clement, the bishop of Rome, to be authoritative. Historical criticism of the Bible was invented and developed primarily by Christian biblical scholars to clarify and defend the historicity of much of what is in the Bible.

Much of the old Life-of-Jesus movement, however, was skeptical—not generally skeptical about the existence of Jesus as a person who really lived but often skeptical about what early Christian thinkers and writers said about Jesus. Yet not only ancient writings could be investigated historically: so also could the religious beliefs that underlay particular writings of the Bible. It is not possible to prove the resurrection of Jesus scientifically, yet we can point out that it is striking how committed remarkably diverse Christians were to the belief in Jesus's resurrection, from the earliest times in which people believed in Jesus. In 1 Cor 15:3–11, Paul recounted several

---

2. It is now common to use the abbreviation CE (Common Era) instead of AD (Anno Domini), and BCE (Before the Common Era) instead of BC (Before Christ). Many biblical scholars are Jews, who do not find it appropriate to use the term "Dominus" ("Lord") to designate Jesus. I favor the use of CE and BCE as a legitimate attempt to use neutral terms to identify the two eras we deal with in the study of the Bible.

accounts of appearances of the risen Jesus to various believers, including the appearance to Paul himself (15:8), in which Paul was commissioned as an apostle.

It is beyond doubt that the historical Jesus was born, that he grew up, that he was a disciple-gathering teacher, and that he went to Jerusalem at the end of his life, where he was arrested, put on trial, and executed by crucifixion by the Roman occupation government in Judea. It is appropriate to study and to debate what Jesus taught, as well as how he taught it. Jesus was a teacher who stood in one or more of the traditions of Judaism, including the tradition of prophets like Elijah and Elisha, as well as the apocalyptic tradition, which encompasses literature like the book of Daniel and (later) the Revelation to John. Thus, Jesus was very much a teacher who attracted a following within Judaism. So was John the Baptizer.

Scholars know now, if they did not fully realize it before the Dead Sea Scrolls were discovered and published, that Judaism in Jesus's time was an extremely diverse phenomenon. The first-century historian Josephus wrote about Judaism as having four sects: the Pharisees, the Sadducees, the Zealots, and the Essenes. It is now believed that there were several groups of Essenes in Israel during the Roman occupation, and that the Dead Sea Scrolls community at Qumran was one such group. It is believed that there was likely an Essene quarter in Jerusalem. Several scholars have argued and do hold that John the Baptizer was an Essene. Thus, to make another long story short, our understanding today of Judaism in the Second Temple period (that is, between the late sixth century BCE and 70 CE) is much more nuanced and better informed than it was before the Dead Sea Scrolls were found in 1947 and were subsequently published, translated, and understood by biblical scholars.

The Synoptic Problem

Undoubtedly the most important thing anyone can do in relation to the Gospels in the New Testament is to read them either in their original language or in an accurate translation. People who have read the Gospels are aware that there are many similarities among the Gospels associated with the names Matthew, Mark, Luke, and John. Matthew and Luke have stories about the virginal conception of Jesus while Mark does not. Yet when Matthew, Mark, and Luke are carefully compared, only some thirty verses of Mark have no equivalents in Matthew and Luke. Matthew and Luke also have around 230 verses in common that Mark does not have. John seems to be significantly different from Matthew, Mark, and Luke in several ways. Both the similarities and the differences have been intensely studied by biblical scholars, going as far back as the late second century of the Common Era. St. Augustine of Hippo, who wrote many books on theology, wrote a book *De consensu evangelistarum* (published in English as *The Harmony of the Gospels*). He decided that Matthew was written first, and that it was a source for Mark. Mark he characterized as a *breviator* ("abbreviator") and *pedisequus* ("foot-follower" or perhaps "protégé") of Matthew.[3] This teaching of St. Augustine was very influential. Other scholars, notably Christian Hermann Weisse in 1838, argued persuasively that Mark was first, and that Matthew and Luke used Mark as a written source. That theory, that Mark was written first and that Matthew and Luke used Mark as a written source, is called "Markan priority." After B. H. Streeter's famous book *The Four Gospels: A Study of Origins, Treating of the Manuscript Tradition, Sources, Authorship, & Dates* was published in 1924, the theory of Markan priority came to be the most commonly accepted theory in the English-speaking world of how Matthew, Mark, and Luke came to be written in relation to each other.[4] Other scholars in the early nineteenth century noted how different the Gospel according to John was in comparison to the other three gospels. Matthew, Mark, and Luke are so similar to each other that these three Gospels are called the Synoptic Gospels.[5] The question of which of them was written first and was a written source for the other two Gospels is called the Synoptic problem. This problem has been intensively studied and debated. The reason this problem has been so important in biblical studies is that the Life-of-Jesus movement in scholarship taught scholars to look for the earliest witness to what Jesus said and did and what Jesus was like. The earlier the witness or source, the closer this witness or source was (and is) to the time of Jesus himself. The likelihood is that the closer in time the

3. Augustine of Hippo, *De consensu evangelistarum* (*The Harmony of the Gospels*) 1.1.4.

4. Streeter's book was published in 1924. It was the definitive statement in English of what became the most accepted solution to the synoptic problem, including the priority of Mark and the existence of another source known as the "synoptic sayings source" or "Q."

5. *Synoptic* means "viewed together." We frequently study the Synoptic Gospels in a book called a synopsis, the most famous of which is Kurt Aland's *Synopsis of the Four Gospels: English Edition*. It is a translation, using the second edition of the Revised Standard Version of the Gospels, of Aland's *Synopsis Quattuor Evangeliorum*, which is now in its fifteenth edition.

source or witness was to what Jesus did and said, the more likely this source or witness conveyed accurate information. Conversely, the later the source or witness, the more likely that extraneous information got into the chain of tradition. So, the impetus that historians have always had to look for primary sources is fundamentally the same impetus to look for the earliest sources. We are looking for the most accurate information about Jesus that we can possibly obtain. This is why we have to be careful, indeed exacting, about the sources we use.

Our interest in sorting through and trying to understand sources in the Gospels is based on the observation by many readers that the Gospels do in fact convey to their readers a diversity of information about Jesus. Sometimes this diversity of information is contradictory. For example, how many times did the adult Jesus go to Jerusalem? In the Synoptic Gospels, Jesus went to Jerusalem once; in the Gospel According to John he went three times. When did Jesus institute the Eucharist? At the Last Supper, according to Matthew, Mark, and Luke, in addition to Paul.[6] In John, Jesus did not institute the Eucharist then (or at all): he did, however, wash his disciples' feet.[7]

Thus, the most important observation we can make about the Gospels, including both the Synoptic Gospels and the Gospel According to John, is that they convey to their readers some information about the life and ministry of Jesus that is the same, much information that is similar, and some information that is characterized by differences. This is not a bad thing. This is the situation that we often find in ancient writings when there are multiple sources describing the same person or the same event. Our task is to understand both the similarities and the differences. Both are important to us.

Who Wrote the Gospel According to Mark?

This may at first seem to be a strange question. Why not simply assume that somebody named Mark wrote the Gospel According to Mark? The reason is that this starting point would be considerably too simple to fit the facts as they are known. Most New Testament scholars believe or at least assume that the Gospels of Matthew, Mark, Luke, and John were originally anonymous. This is my belief. There are bits and pieces of evidence that suggest

6. Matt 26:26–39; Mark 14:22–25; Luke 22:15–20; 1 Corinthians 11:23–26.
7. John 13:1–20.

otherwise, yet there are perennial questions that surround this fragmentary information, so that it is difficult for anyone to know what the evidence actually means. I will unpack briefly what the problem is with being confident that someone named Mark composed or otherwise formulated the gospel we know as Mark.

First, within the actual Greek text of Mark that we have, based on many ancient manuscripts, there is no mention the name of any author, even though most manuscripts identify the book as (the Gospel) According to Mark. Since the manuscripts of this gospel that we have do not mention sa person named Mark (or anybody else) who was its author, we are on solid ground when we consider the Gospel According to Mark to be an anonymous work. Someone did write Mark in the first century CE, but we do not have any hard evidence as to who this author was. A great deal of church tradition identifies the author as Mark who was associated with the apostle Peter. Unfortunately, this tradition from the early church is hard to interpret, since we cannot be certain what particular text Christian writers of the second and third centuries CE were referring to when they mentioned a gospel associated with Mark. If some writers were referring to a Gospel According to Mark that is generally the same as the one we know, we have no assurance that other writers, perhaps in other regions of the church, were referring to the same document. Hence, we are justified in being quite careful about the issue of the authorship of the Gospel According to Mark. I will simply refer to the author of the Gospel According to Mark as Mark, by virtue of the fact that the name Mark has been conventionally used to indicate the author of that gospel as well as the short title of the gospel itself. Despite this use of Mark as both the author and the title of the gospel, it is not known who the author of Mark was, because there is no hard evidence from the first century CE that would tell us.

I do prefer the title The Gospel According to Mark. Note that in this traditional title, the word "gospel" is in the singular. The term *gospel* in the singular is also the way the earliest Christian writer, Paul, used it. Paul did not think that the word "gospel" was the title or the genre of written biographical works about Jesus. Paul understood the gospel to be the saving message of who Jesus was and what Jesus did, especially including his death and resurrection.[8] The gospel was what Paul preached and taught.

---

8. See especially 1 Corinthians 15:1 and 9:18, as well as Hughes, "Gospel and Its Rhetoric in Galatians."

Why These Questions Are Important

And so we come back to the most important question of all: Why have those who study the Bible spent so much time and effort asking questions about how and when biblical texts were composed, who wrote them, and what these writers had in mind? You could ask this question: Why shouldn't we read the Gospels purely for their spiritual value and inspiration for us twenty-first-century readers? The reason we cannot is that those of us who study the Bible and, as I believe, especially the New Testament, want to know, as certainly as we can know, what really happened. It makes a difference what Jesus really did. It makes a difference what Paul taught about the death and resurrection of Christ and about justification. Despite several problems with the study of the historical Jesus, we still have the intellectual curiosity (if not also the chutzpah) to want to know the real human story behind the written text. We want to know what Jesus was like, including what he taught and what he did. To be perfectly honest, I think that people who are in the Christian family should want to know these things more strongly than anyone else might want to know them. But as believers or not, we can agree that Jesus and what he said and did are important parts of the cultural heritages of the world in which we now live. As a Christian and as a priest and teacher, I am deeply committed to learning everything I can about Jesus, including what can be learned by reading and studying the Gospels of the New Testament.

And so this brings us again to the question of why one should study the Gospel According to Mark. My belief is that Jesus was born in Bethlehem, was raised in Nazareth as a believing and practicing Jew, and was taught about the Torah and the Prophets by his parents and by his local rabbis. Jesus was in no way an outsider to Judaism. He was not anti-Jewish in the least. Jesus did during his ministry enter into various debates that were in fact Jewish debates dealing with the faith and practices of Judaism. One may doubt that Jesus's controversy with the Sadducees in Mark 12:18–27 (with its parallels Matt 22:23–33 and Luke 20:27–40), in which the Sadducees asked Jesus a trick question about the resurrection, was the first time Jesus discussed the afterlife with other Jews, either in a synagogue school taught by his local rabbi or in other contexts. Jesus's context within Judaism in Galilee has been the subject of study by learned scholars including Géza Vermes, and one need not agree with everything that Vermes has argued in *Jesus the Jew* in order to appreciate the commitment and care that

Vermes and others have shown in their investigation of the Jewish context of the Gospels.

In addition to the spirituality of Mark within its Jewish context, it is important to note that as the earliest of the four Gospels to have been written, Mark makes a great contribution to the spiritualities of Christians, and it has done so for a long time. For one thing, Mark doesn't waste even a drop of ink in telling the readers how wonderful or smart the apostles, in this gospel often called the Twelve, are. The author of Mark actually seems to have the opposite view of the apostles. Mark seems perfectly fearless about describing for the readers the fact that the Twelve generally don't understand the meaning of some of Jesus's parables, so that Jesus has to explain their meaning to the apostles privately (Mark 4:34). Then there is the whole question of the faithfulness of the Twelve to Jesus when the going gets rough. After Jesus is arrested by the group of soldiers assigned to the chief priest, the apostles flee. Not only that, but when confronted by outsiders accusing him of association with the Jesus, who was then in Roman custody, Peter denies his association with Jesus not merely once but three times, which Jesus himself predicts (Mark 14:72 and 14:30). Thus, many if not most readers of Mark recognize that Peter and the other apostles are not generally portrayed in a favorable light—not only in the narrative of the suffering and death of Christ but also elsewhere in the gospel.

The relatively negative portrayals of the apostles in Mark can be read in different ways. One way is simply to take these often negative images of the apostles at face value, as an attack by the writer of Mark on the original apostles of Jesus. Another way to read the negative images of the apostles, however, is for us to reason that since Peter denies Jesus but later repents and becomes the leader of twelve Spirit-filled emissaries of Christ, we as Christians can trust that before us are the possibilities of both sinning and repenting. Like people in all walks of life, those who are followers of Christ—even including those in his inner circle of disciples—can make grave mistakes but can also learn from those mistakes in order to act in right ways in the future. So, a legitimate way to read about the apostles' foibles in Mark is to interpret them within the larger picture of (hopefully) our general faithfulness to Christ. Or to put it briefly: Peter could repent and change—and you and I can repent and change. That is good news.

Something else can be said about the portrayals of people in the Gospel of Mark. They are not sugarcoated. They are real. Mark shows the apostles as real people who have massive trouble both understanding who

Jesus is and also resolving how they should live their lives, having known Jesus before his death and resurrection. The women who visit the empty tomb in Mark 16:1–8 are doing so to anoint the dead body of Jesus. Not only are they not expecting Jesus to be raised from death; when told of Jesus's resurrection, they do not believe it. The earliest and best manuscripts of Mark end at 16:8, which we may translate as follows: "Indeed going out of the tomb, they fled; trembling and astonishment had overtaken them; and they said nothing to anyone, for they were afraid."

How to Study the Gospels

Christians should study the Gospels of the New Testament. I believe any person who wants to understand the cultures of the world would want to read and study the Gospels. Thus we can now turn to the question of how to study the Gospels.

Reading an accurate translation of the Gospel According to Mark is an excellent and necessary start. After reading Mark in one or two sittings, as recommended, readers will very likely begin to form images their minds. These images will probably include pictures of what Jesus was like and also of what the author of the Gospel According to Mark was like. Other images may well include what Jesus's disciples were like, how they dealt with Jesus and with his teaching and ministry, and how they dealt with each other. Do not worry about these images or the fact that some of them may be either thought-provoking or downright troubling. Biblical texts can elicit some perplexing reactions!

Students of the Gospels have generally read them in one of several ways. First, if we do not know the Greek of the New Testament, usually called Hellenistic or Koiné Greek, it is desirable to start with a really good translation. Several excellent translations come to mind: the New Revised Standard Version (NRSV), the New Revised Version Updated Edition (NRSVue), the New International Version (NIV), the New American Bible (NAB), the New Jerusalem Bible (NJB), as well as the older Revised Standard Version (RSV). Since our knowledge of both the biblical languages (Hebrew, Aramaic, and Greek) and of biblical authors and editors continues to grow year by year, it is not a good idea to read any translation made before the twentieth century. In the case of the New Testament, we want to have an accurate translation made from an edition of the Greek text that takes into account the approximately 5,700 manuscripts of all or part of the

New Testament. Most of these manuscripts were unavailable to the translators of the Bible in the seventeenth century, so while we should honor the translators of the King James Version for doing an excellent job with the texts they had to work with, scholars now know that we have a much more accurate Greek text to translate than they did. Instead of dealing with the Greek text that circulated in the tenth and later centuries of our era, when we use the current editions of what's called the Nestle-Aland *Novum Testamentum Graece* or the United Bible Societies' *The Greek New Testament*, we are generally dealing with the text that was circulating in the early church in the fourth century, with some manuscripts going back to the end of the second century. Thus, our current critical editions of the New Testament in ancient Greek are fundamentally a great advance over the Greek texts that the King James translators and their predecessors used or could have used. I have been a priest since 1981, and from my pastoral experience I can also attest that it is important that the translations of the Bible be made into a form of the English language that people who are alive now can actually read and understand. From my Anglican tradition I can cite Article XXIV of the Thirty-Nine Articles of Religion, from the sixteenth century of our era, which stated it very well: "It is a thing plainly repugnant to the Word of God, and the custom of the Primitive Church, to have public Prayer in the church, or to minister the Sacraments, in a tongue not understanded of the people." If it is "plainly repugnant" to have public prayers and celebrations of the sacraments in a language foreign to the people, what would be the point of reading a translation of the Bible that was written in an archaic form of the English language? I do not believe there is any. Why bother to use an English translation of the Bible that most English-speaking people cannot now understand? I cannot think of any good reason to do so. Nostalgia is not a good reason.

The Bible is notable for many reasons. So many passages and books in the Bible have the ability not only to inform us but also to inspire us and to comfort us when we need inspiration or comfort. Yet an important aspect of Scripture, in both testaments, is that it has an uncanny ability to challenge us—to make us aware of the uncomfortable messages of the prophets of the Hebrew Bible as well as the uncomfortable messages of a later prophet (namely, John the Baptizer) along with the teaching of Jesus, which was often challenging and difficult to hear. The apostle Paul took up that mantle when he wrote the letter we know as 2 Cor 10:1—13:13, after he had been rejected as the apostle of the church in Corinth, when he made his second visit to the church, to straighten its members out, and was then rejected as the church's apostle. The book of Revelation, at the end of the New Testament, has more often than not been misunderstood, and that misunderstanding has resulted in bizarre books such as Hal Lindsay's *The Late Great Planet Earth*, which was given a spirited refutation in Robert Jewett's *Jesus Against the Rapture*. Thus readers of the Bible either are or will get used to readings of the Bible which are challenging and, at times, troubling.

Mark's treatment of the followers of Jesus is, to my mind, troubling. The Jesus of Mark is not at all picky about whom he chooses as his closest followers, whom Mark seems to prefer calling the Twelve instead of apostles or disciples. In Mark neither the women nor the Twelve are witnesses to Jesus's resurrection, since in 16:1–8 they don't expect it or believe it when it is told to them. This, in my estimation, is the most troubling aspect of Mark.

So, for many reasons, the Gospel According to Mark is intriguing. It clearly has a point of view concerning the disciples of Jesus as well as other characters. This point of view is generally negative. The Twelve just don't "get" Jesus. Jesus even has to explain his parables privately to them, precisely because they do not understand them (4:34).

What does this tale of the Twelve's repeated lack of understanding tell either the ancient or modern reader? Perhaps it increases the interest the readers were expected to have in Jesus, so that readers are to think, "The Twelve didn't understand Jesus, but if I persevere reading this gospel, hopefully I can understand him and hopefully I will become a good follower of Jesus." Yet the Gospel According to Mark is subtle. The meanings of Mark sometimes appear obvious, but it is more like the writer of Mark is trying to invite the reader to become a follower of Jesus. Perhaps Schweitzer had it right as he concluded *The Quest of the Historical Jesus* with these words: "He commands. And to those who hearken to him, whether wise or unwise, he will reveal himself in the peace, the labours, the conflicts and the suffering that they may experience in his fellowship, and as an ineffable mystery they will learn who he is."[9] Yet it truly is possible to understand the Gospel According to Mark by carefully reading it. Readers of Mark probably will not agree what every sentence or each detail of this gospel means, yet the broad outlines of the perspective and meaning of Mark should be clear. As I write this guide, I am working to make Mark's Gospel understandable to readers.

---

9. Schweitzer, *Quest of the Historical Jesus*, 487.

2

Introducing the Gospel According to Mark

Mark 1:1–15

The "Big Picture" of Mark

BEFORE WE LOOK AT particular passages of the Gospel According to Mark, it would be helpful to identify the most important themes and other features found in Mark. The following points are essential elements of what I call the "big picture" of Mark. By "big picture," I mean the overall message of Mark that the author wished to make sure that the readers of this book would not miss. I identify these elements as follows:

1. The impending and present intervention of God in the life of people living in Israel in the early first century of the Common Era (CE). This intervention consisted of sending Jesus of Nazareth not only to announce but to inaugurate God's kingdom or reign. The coming and ministry of Jesus's forerunner, John the Baptizer, was also part of the intervention of God.

2. The person of Jesus, who was the Son of God. For Mark, as well as the other gospel writers, Jesus's miracles function to show readers that Jesus was able to do miracles all through his adult life. Thus, the miracle stories in Mark reveal to readers that Jesus was able to do what

ordinary human beings were and are unable to do. Thus, Jesus's miracles, as they are presented in Mark and the other gospels, are strongly christological. They are illustrations and examples of the person and power of Jesus.

3. The plotting against Jesus (including both the public and secret undermining by various Jewish leaders), his arrest, and his trial, resulting in the torturous execution by crucifixion under the auspices of the Roman occupation government. Despite this opposition, which, according to Mark, resulted in Jesus's death, he nonetheless remained Son of God.

4. The inability of Jesus's earliest followers to comprehend fully, if at all, the nature of Jesus's ministry—a misunderstanding that culminated in their abandonment of Jesus during his passion and death, as well as in their lack of faith in Jesus's resurrection even when it was both predicted by Jesus himself three times and proclaimed to them by an angel at the tomb of Jesus, which, to their great surprise, did not contain his body.

5. The paradoxical facts that Jesus was the Messiah and that Jewish people in Israel generally did not recognize or accept Jesus as the Messiah.

6. The strong connections between Jesus and various prophets of the Hebrew Bible, starting with the opening quotations from Malachi and Isaiah, and continuing with notable intertextual interaction between Jesus and the Elijah/Elisha cycle of miracle stories found in 1 Kgs 17 through 2 Kgs 13.[1]

7. The nature of the kingdom of God, which was inaugurated by the person and work of Jesus, and which will be fully realized when Jesus makes his second coming.

8. The cause of God's intervention: the flagrant and many-faceted offenses against justice committed by human beings against God and against other human beings. Human beings sin, both against God and each other. Hatred within and among nations flourishes. Left to its own devices, humanity has been shown to be perpetually unable to right many of the wrongs in the world.

---

1. The strong identification of the intertextuality between the Elijah/Elisha cycle of stories and the John the Baptizer/Jesus stories in Mark has been made in Roth, *Hebrew Gospel*, 1–20.

9. The portrayal of Jesus primarily as a healer and secondarily as a teacher. Jesus generally teaches by speaking to crowds in parables.
10. The orders that Jesus frequently gave to remain silent about the healing miracles that he had just then performed. Paradoxically, these orders, known to epitomize what New Testament scholars call "the messianic secret," were usually disobeyed.

It is important to take note of how paradoxical several of these elements of Mark's presentation of Jesus are, including Jesus's ministry, his message, and the reception of his message by his earliest followers. To put it in the simplest terms, Mark presents Jesus in remarkably positive ways, and generally Jesus's disciples are presented in remarkably negative ways. Thus, the author of Mark was telling the original readers of this gospel not only about God the Father and Jesus of Nazareth, but also about Jesus's message of the kingdom of God. Along with what Mark says about God, Jesus, and the kingdom, it is not hard to identify Mark's significantly negative view of the church that existed in the middle to late first century CE.

As this book proceeds, I will comment on these ten elements, the foundations of Mark's thought. For now, however, I want to give the readers of this book a summary of what I am going to argue in favor of. Mark is far from a primitive or simple book. It has its own distinctive way of looking at things. Other people who wrote books in the ancient world had their points of view as well. Wolfgang Roth's provocative book *Hebrew Gospel* explores in detail the relationship between Mark and the Elijah/Elisha cycle of stories found between 1 Kgs 17 and 2 Kgs 13 in the Hebrew Bible / Old Testament. Mark made the partial though deeply symbolic identification of John the Baptizer with Elijah and of Jesus with Elisha. Thus, it is no accident that just as Elijah and especially Elisha did many miracles, so Jesus as presented in Mark also is a very prolific performer of miracles. (In the Gospel According to John, in contrast, Jesus does seven miracles; each time Jesus does a miracle in John he preaches about the meaning of each miracle for a chapter or two.) Indeed, miracles and miracle stories are well established parts of the oral tradition about Jesus. This oral tradition was eventually transformed into the Gospels as we know them. Among the writers of the Gospels, the writer of Mark was the first to make this transformation. We should read the Gospel According to Mark as a pioneering written work. It both presents Jesus and encourages faith in Jesus in an uncompromising way. It shows Jesus as following Jewish tradition in a number of ways, particularly the prophetic tradition—and, perhaps following the prophetic tradition as well, the writer of Mark shows Jewish people, particularly Jewish leaders in Jerusalem under Roman occupation during Jesus's lifetime, as generally unreceptive to what Jesus was doing. The writers of the four New Testament Gospels cast most of the blame for the death of Jesus on those Jewish leaders, yet the historical fact is that the Roman occupation government headed by Pontius Pilate in the Roman province of Judaea was completely responsible for Jesus's death.[2]

Mark 1:1–15

The first fifteen verses of the Gospel According to Mark set the tone for the rest of Mark. The very first verse, Mark 1:1, seems to have been the original title of this written work: "the good news of Jesus Christ [Son of God]." Neither these first fifteen verses nor any other verses in Mark mention anything about the author of this work. The "gospel" mentioned in 1:1 is the "official message" or "good news" concerning Jesus Christ. Many manuscripts add "Son of God" in 1:1, and it is possible that these words were an original part of this verse of Mark. Readers should pay careful attention to the fact that no expression anywhere in the text of Mark suggests that it belongs to a literary genre called a gospel. Mark, along with the other New Testament gospels, would have been understood in antiquity as consistent with the well-known genre of biography.

Greek biographies typically indicated the origin of the person about whom the biography was written. In Mark there is no narrative of the birth, infancy, or childhood of Jesus, yet there is a considerable amount of material in 1:2–11 about John the Baptizer, who is somehow the forerunner of Jesus. Quite unlike the narrative in Luke (see 1:36), Mark does not offer any identification of John the Baptizer as a relative of Jesus, however distant. In Mark 1:2–3 there are quotations of two passages from the Greek Old Testament,[3] from Mal 3:1 and Isa 40:3 (although both quotations are identified as from "Isaiah the prophet" in 1:2). In the absence of any information describing the ancestry, parentage, or birth of Jesus, the quotations from Malachi and Isaiah identify John the Baptizer in important ways. The readers will come to learn that John is the forerunner of Jesus, but the context

---

2. Gnilka, *Jesus of Nazareth*, 301.

3. This version of the Greek Old Testament is usually called the Septuagint (abbreviated as LXX) or the Old Greek.

of the quotation from Mal 3:1 shows that the one who is the "messenger" sent "ahead of your face" is the forerunner of none other than God. In Mark 1:3 John the Baptizer is described as the one who is "in the wilderness" to "prepare the way of the Lord," and the reader will learn that "the Lord" in this case is Jesus. So these two quotations from Malachi and Isaiah are significant both for the identification of John the Baptizer and also for the identification of Jesus, who, as the readers will learn in 1:9-11, is Son of God and who will often be addressed as *Kyrios*, meaning not merely "sir" but "Lord" in the sense that it is usually employed in the Greek Old Testament—that is, as a title and form of address for God.

In 1:4-8 the reader learns the nature of the preparation that John the Baptizer did for the life and ministry of Jesus. John was a preacher who started a renewal movement within Judaism, encouraging repentance from his fellow Jews. The Dead Sea Scrolls, discovered near Khirbet Qumran in 1947 and published in subsequent years, clearly demonstrate that John was not the only leader within Judaism who advocated a radical form of repentance, including the confession of personal sins by those who entered the movement and those who remained in the movement. Like the prophets of the Hebrew Bible in the eighth and seventh centuries BCE, and like the sectarian Jews of the Dead Sea Scrolls community, John the Baptizer called those who heard his preaching to repentance: to confess past and present sins and to live holy lives. Like the Qumran community and like the prophet Elijah, John the Baptizer lived in the wilderness rather than in a house in a town. The Qumran community was founded and led by a person known in the Dead Sea Scrolls as the "Teacher of Righteousness" or the "Righteous Teacher." And similar to the perspective of the Qumran writings—particularly of what's known as the War Scroll (1QM)[4]—John the Baptizer preached about a divine intervention in the future, in which sinners would be punished and the righteous would be rewarded. Jesus and Paul shared this perspective. Some scholars identify John the Baptizer as an Essene, as the members of the Qumran community were.[5] Thus, it appears that both John the Baptizer and adherents of this strand of Judaism in the Second Temple period held ideas in common, including especially God's coming intervention in the lives of Jewish people. Before this cosmic or

---

4. See the translation by Florentino García Martínez, *Dead Sea Scrolls Translated*, 95-125.

5. Against the view that John the Baptizer was an Essene, see the critical examination of the evidence in Hartmut Stegemann, *Library of Qumran*, 211-27.

earthly intervention that God was planning, Jewish people, it was believed, needed to prepare by confessing their sins and by living sanctified lives. Mark 1:5 tells its readers that "people from the whole Judean countryside and all the people of Jerusalem" came out to where John the Baptizer was, as he preached and baptized people in the Jordan River. Thus, John's renewal movement, culminating in fellow Jews' confessing their sins and getting baptized by John, must have been a significant influence, even if "all the people of Jerusalem" (a clearly exaggerated phrase) did not actually come to the Jordan for John's baptism. Additionally, there are parallels between John the Baptizer and the prophet Elijah, as found in 2 Kgs 1:8; they were what many of us today would call "outdoorsy."[6] It is not too much to say about John the Baptizer that he did not fit in well with the leadership of Judaism in Israel or, for that matter, with people who spent most of their life in buildings. Like the Essenes at the Dead Sea, John rejected most of what was conventional in Judaism, in favor of his own much more severe, back-to-nature lifestyle.

Very notably, what John says of himself is that one is coming "more powerful than I" and that "I am not worthy to stoop down and untie the thong of his sandals" (1:7). Thus, just like Elijah was the forerunner of Elisha, John the Baptizer is the forerunner of Jesus of Nazareth. This quite explicitly presents John and Jesus according to the scriptural model found in the Elijah/Elisha cycle of stories from the Former Prophets. So following the scriptural model of Elijah and Elisha, the Gospel According to Mark begins to tell the story of Jesus by basing it on the story of John the Baptizer. And we can remember from Mark 1:2–3 that the whole picture of John the Baptizer as the "messenger ahead of your face, who will prepare your way" (cf. Mal 3:1) and who is "the voice of one shouting in the wilderness" to "prepare the way of the Lord" and "make his paths straight" (cf. Isa 40:3) is based on other scriptural texts from the Latter Prophets. These scriptural warrants from both the Former and Latter Prophets in the Hebrew Bible (Old Testament) serve to heighten the awareness of Mark's reader that something akin to what the prophets of old foretold was happening in the lifetimes and ministries of John the Baptizer and Jesus. The pairs of Elijah and Elisha (on the one hand) and John and Jesus (on the other) were deeply and personally involved in the renewal—indeed the transformation—of the relationship between God and the people of God. God was doing a new

---

6. Roth, *Hebrew Gospel*, 93: "Mark's description of John the Baptist in 1:6 alludes clearly to that of Elijah in 2 Kgs 1:8 (comp. Mk 9:9–11)."

thing as John preached repentance and baptized, and as Jesus preached and taught about the kingdom of God and did his many miracles.

The baptism of Jesus is presented in 1:9–11. This passage in Mark is rather shorter than its parallel in Matt 3:13–17 and about the same length as its parallel in Luke 3:21–22. The baptism of Jesus is a unique event in the Gospels. Although baptism is the unique and unrepeatable rite in which Christians are initiated into the Christian faith and life, the baptism of Jesus consisted of something quite different. Jesus did not need to be initiated into anything: he was a circumcised and practicing Jewish man. The baptism of Jesus, as it is presented in Mark and its parallels, was therefore not an initiation rite, but a rite in which God the Father officially recognized Jesus as the Son of God. The "sound from the heavens" proclaimed in the second person singular, "You are my Son, the beloved one; in you I am well pleased" (1:11 my trans.). In the Gospels According to Matthew and Luke, infancy narratives about Jesus make it clear to readers that he is uniquely the Son of God and not the biological son of Joseph. In Mark there is no such a narrative concerning either the parentage of Jesus or the virginity of his mother, Mary; neither is anything at all said in Mark about Joseph. The baptism of Jesus identifies for Mark's readers that Jesus is God's Son. The two scriptures quoted in 1:2–3, namely Mal 3:1 and especially Isa 40:3, establish the identify of John the Baptizer as the forerunner of "the Lord." So the identity of Jesus as "the Lord" is already buttressed by Scripture, in that Jesus's "way" will be "the way of the Lord" (1:3) The baptism of Jesus in 1:9–11 gives the reader a complete confirmation of Jesus's divine status. The ceremony of baptism, in which it was proclaimed by none other than the voice of God that Jesus was divine in that he is Son of God, will become the essential initiation rite for followers of Jesus. God says that Jesus is his Son in 1:11. Yet even before that, in 1:7–8, John the Baptizer testifies concerning Jesus that he is "mightier" than John and that John is "not worthy to untie the thong of his sandals" (1:7). Jesus also "will baptize you with the Holy Spirit" (1:8).

John the Baptizer, we have learned (1:3–4, etc.), is "in the wilderness." After his baptism by John, Jesus also spends "forty days" in the wilderness (1:12–13) where he underwent temptations. Jesus was "with the animals." Given that Jesus has been identified as Son of God (1:11), his divine status makes it appropriate that "angels ministered to him." Perhaps this mitigates the vulnerability and thus the humility that the newly baptized Jesus would have had in the wilderness. Instead of needing to hunt and forage for food, as others would have to do in the wilderness, Jesus as Son of God has food provided for him by the angels. We are not told about where Jesus slept at night during the wilderness testing. If he was "with the animals," he apparently was kept safe from animal attacks, presumably also by angels. Mark does not provide any details of exactly what the angels did to minister to Jesus. Why does Jesus go into the wilderness? He is "thrown out into the wilderness" (1:12) by the Holy Spirit which had come "upon him" at his baptism (1:10). The purpose of the temptations, which are done by Satan, is to toughen Jesus up, making him ready for spiritual battles which will be frequent in Mark, especially in the many healing miracles Jesus will perform, which are fundamentally exorcisms of evil or "unclean" spirits. Since diseases were believed to be caused by such spirits and demons, Jesus's many healing miracles entailed the casting out of these demons and unclean spirits.

Jesus's ability to cast out evil spirits helps to bring into focus the apparent sinlessness of Jesus. Matt 3:14–15, which asserts quite explicitly for the readers of that gospel the sinlessness of Jesus, a theological idea that one finds elsewhere in the New Testament,[7] contrasts with Mark 1:9–11 and Luke 3:21–22, where the sinlessness of Jesus is not dealt with at all. Yet 1:9 comes in Mark immediately after John the Baptizer has proclaimed that the one "coming after me" "is more powerful than I" and that John the Baptizer himself is unworthy to stoop down so that he could untie the thong of the coming one's sandals. It is correct to say that the sinlessness of Jesus is presupposed in Mark rather than asserted in detail. I will have more to say about the innocence of Jesus as I deal with the passion narrative, including the trial of Jesus.

Mark 1:14 gives rather little attention to John the Baptizer, who essentially drops out of Mark until John's beheading in 6:17–29. The unjust execution of John (in this case the term "murder" is more accurate) can certainly be seen as a foreshadowing of the unjust execution of Jesus in Mark 15:6–47.

This introductory section of Mark opens and closes with extremely significant uses of *euaggelion*, the word we translate as "gospel" or "good news" or "official message."[8] Mark 1:1 seems to identify the whole book as "the gospel of Jesus Christ, the Son of God," yet we readers are not told in

---

7. Most notably 2 Corinthians 5:21 and Hebrews 4:15.

8. The noun *euaggelion* occurs at Mark 1:1; 1:14; 1:15; 8:35; 10:29; 13:10; 14:9; and in the longer ending of Mark at 16:15.

1:1 what the *euaggelion* is. In 1:14, readers are told, "Jesus came to Galilee, proclaiming the *euaggelion* of God." And in 1:15, which is usually thought of as a summary of the proclamation of Jesus, we are told what Jesus was proclaiming: that "the time is fulfilled and the kingdom of God has come near." As the response to the fulfillment of the time and the near approach of the kingdom of God in the coming of Jesus, the original hearers of Jesus are given the command to "repent and believe in the gospel." And so the noun *euaggelion* is twice more in 1:14–15 flashed before the eyes of the reader, now not as at the beginning of the narrative of Mark itself (1:1), but as an invitation, if not a command, to trust in the gospel that comes directly from the life and proclamation of Jesus himself. Nonetheless, by 1:15 there is much more that the reader would like to know about "the gospel." As we read further and further in the Gospel According to Mark, a book which the author or compiler has even identified as "the gospel of Jesus Christ" (1:1), we will see the content and meaning of "the gospel" unfold. Ironically and paradoxically, "the gospel" will unfold by showing the readers in narrative form both the sinlessness of Jesus and also the apostles' failure to grasp the fact, until after Jesus's death at the earliest, that it is through Jesus's death and its effect on believers in Jesus that salvation will be accomplished.

Conclusions

My understanding of Mark 1:1–15 suggests that the original readers of Mark, having not read Matthew or Luke, might ask some questions that Matthew and Luke try to answer. As the reader reads the texts, later in the Gospel of Mark, in which Jesus does so many deeds which demonstrate his mighty power, they would be able to look back at Mark 1:1–15 and take note of the fact that, with John the Baptizer as his forerunner, as prophets in Scripture itself say, and with the divine voice from heaven proclaiming to Jesus, "You are my beloved Son, in whom I am well pleased" (1:11), Jesus did what he did not as John the Baptizer or one of the prophets did, but as Son of God. This would include his deeds of power, his preaching, and finally his passion and death, followed by his resurrection. He could do all these things precisely because he was Son of God, God's beloved. His humanity was proven by his suffering and death. Even his suffering and death, denoting his humanity, were actually foreshadowed in the forty days of temptations in the wilderness (1:12–13). Yet even then as "he was with the animals, angels ministered to him." This suggests that the created order, including wild animals and angels, is fully cognizant of who and what Jesus is. When Jesus does exorcisms, the demons also know who Jesus is. Notably, this knowledge of Jesus's identity as Son of God does not find its way into the consciousness of the apostles, as far as we are told in Mark, until 8:29 when Peter says to Jesus, "You are the Messiah." So the author of the Gospel According to Mark goes out of the way to impress upon the readers of Mark just how much in the dark the Twelve original followers of Jesus truly are about the one whom they are following and listening to. Surely it is clear to us now that this rhetoric about the Twelve is not happenstance! The author of Mark wants to make sure that the readers of Mark understand just what kind of followers Jesus was working with.

That is part and parcel of the rhetoric of Mark. What Mark wrote for the benefit of his readers can be understood in at least two ways. On the one hand, it can be seen as some negative publicity against the apostles from the author of Mark. On the other hand, it can be seen more positively. As readers comprehend the ways in which the earliest apostles of Jesus often failed him, contemporary Jesus-believers can say to themselves, "If Peter and others could fail and still be apostles, I too can fail and still be a follower of Jesus." The failures of Peter and the other early followers of Jesus, both at the levels of understanding and of acting, can give readers of this gospel hope that they too can move beyond their own failures of discipleship and move toward becoming obedient and mature Jesus-believers.[9] At the present moment in North American Christianity, if not also elsewhere, it is clear to me that we Christians could use quite a few significant doses of reality about our own contemporary failures of discipleship, both as individuals and as churches. Mark reminds us that failures of discipleship are by no means confined to our own generation of Jesus-believers. This process of looking back at the first generation of Jesus-believers and their foibles must not be done to excuse our many contemporary failings, but to take them seriously, so that we can create ways to move beyond our failings and to do considerably better in the future.

---

9. On the failures of the Twelve, and the positive way of interpreting them, see Garland, *Theology of Mark's Gospel*, 405–33, especially 407, along with Garland, *Mark*, 137–38. See also Byrne, *Costly Freedom*, as well as Moloney, *Gospel of Mark*, 352–54.

3

Jesus's Ministry in Galilee
Mark 1:16—3:6

THIS SECTION OF MARK begins the presentation of Jesus's ministry in Galilee, the region in which he grew up, in the north of Israel. He has not yet gone to Jerusalem, according to this Gospel.

Fishing for People

Mark tells its readers that Jesus went by the Sea of Galilee and saw several men who were fishermen and asked them to come and follow him. Without conveying any information about where they were going to go and what they were going to do, and how and where they were going to find food, eat, and sleep, Jesus successfully calls Simon and his brother Andrew (1:16-18) and then, going a little farther, calls James and his brother John, the sons of Zebedee (1:19-20). As we have already noted, the author of Mark has few if any positive thoughts about the apostles. From the perspective of the Gospel According to Mark, the apostles have two major problems: they are not very intelligent, and they are unfaithful to Jesus when he is arrested. As I read Mark 1:16-20, it is reasonable to acknowledge a connection between Jesus's apparent lack of care in choosing his twelve apostles (one of them being Judas Iscariot, Mark 3:19; 14:10, 43) and the negative images of the apostles elsewhere in Mark, about which much has been written.[1]

---

1. See Kingsbury, *Conflict in Mark*, especially 89-117.

The unusual phrase "I will make you fish for people" (1:17) gives more than a hint of what Jesus wants the Twelve to do when he finishes training them to be *apostoloi* ("apostles," meaning "those who are sent out"). The Twelve are going to "go fishing" for people. They had years of training and experience at fishing for fish—this was how they and their fathers had made their living. Yet now the object of their ministry of attraction was not going to be fish but people. This is what we currently call evangelism. The band of Jesus's followers had Jesus not only as its leader but as a focus or goal: to "fish" for and hopefully to catch people. At this point in Mark, readers are not told that the people the Twelve will be attracting will be anybody other than fellow Jews.

Miracle Stories

After the first four followers of Jesus have been called, this group of men goes to a city on the northern shore of the Sea of Galilee, Capernaum. On the Sabbath, Jesus enters the local synagogue and teaches (1:21). There is "a man with an unclean spirit," meaning that he is possessed by a demon. The demon in the man recognizes that Jesus is "the Holy One of God," evidently meaning that the demon recognizes Jesus as the Messiah, the Anointed One. The demon also recognizes that Jesus has power over him. Jesus first silences the demon and then casts the demon out of the afflicted man. As the demon exits the man (and readers of this story are not told where the demon goes), he convulsed the afflicted man. The witnesses to this exorcism, which is in fact a healing miracle, comment favorably on Jesus's teaching and his authority over unclean spirits (1:27). This "immediately" causes Jesus to be talked about in that region of Galilee (1:28). Jesus thus becomes a famous person there.

Form criticism of the Gospels fundamentally began with the famous work of Karl Ludwig Schmidt, *The Framework of the Story of Jesus*, which was published in German in 1919 and in English translation in 2021. Schmidt argued quite persuasively that stories found in the Gospel According to Mark originally existed as separate units rather than as an originally continuous narrative. This is not hard to believe. An important corollary of what Schmidt argued is the similarity of miracle stories in the Synoptic Gospels with other miracle stories in the wider Hellenistic culture. Rudolf Bultmann demonstrated this by means of parallels in *The History of the Synoptic Tradition*, published in German in 1921 and in English translation in 1963. The many parallels suggest that miracle stories had a lively and popular existence in Jesus-believing circles, as well as in other circles in late antiquity, for several years before the Gospels as we now know them were written down. In other words, many of the narratives of the deeds of power that Jesus performed appear to have been formed as oral stories before they were written down as miracle stories in Mark, Matthew, Luke, John, or any of the other, noncanonical gospels of which we are aware.

The story in 1:23–28 is a miracle story. Miracle stories are included in the New Testament Gospels to illustrate the power and authority of Jesus to do deeds of power that normally human beings are unable to do. They show that during Jesus's earthly life, which eventually he would voluntarily give up after his arrival in Jerusalem with his disciples, as we read in the passion narrative of Mark 14:1—15:47, Jesus performed deeds of power. The author of Mark is presenting readers with the perspective that Jesus's power to do the miraculous was not characteristic only of his new life after resurrection from death; he did deeds of power just as Elijah and Elisha did, during his life before his death and resurrection. Thus, the miracle stories are important as details of Jesus's life; yet their greater importance to the theology and rhetoric of Mark is that Jesus, not only after his resurrection but also during his natural life, was able and willing to do deeds of power for the benefit of people who needed his help.[2] These stories not only speak of Jesus's power to perform miracles but also to his compassion and love for people whom he had never met before. Thus, they tell the readers of Jesus's power and spiritual authority, and they are part of the Christian tradition, with strong roots in Jewish tradition: through these miracle stories, followers of Jesus, human beings as they are, are given examples of divine and human compassion to follow.

Miracle stories had a characteristic form.[3] This form is believed to have had its origin in the oral telling of stories about Jesus, such oral storytelling

---

2. Bultmann, *Synoptic Tradition*, 218–19.

3. On miracle stories, the most important works of form criticism include Dibelius, *From Tradition*, 70–103; Bultmann, *Synoptic Tradition*, 209–44. Much has been written for and against form criticism of the Synoptic Gospels; to some extent this is because form criticism of the Gospels allows scholars to raise anew the question of whether particular passages in the Gospels reflect historical events or are simply literary creations. I look on form criticism of the Gospels as an honest and honorable attempt to reconstruct much of the process of how oral sayings of Jesus became written stories in the Gospels. It must be said that form criticism of the Gospels has been practiced in a variety of ways. Form criticism as practiced by Dibelius and Bultmann had its roots in the classic work of Schmidt, *Framework*. For recent critiques of form criticism of the Gospels, see Keener,

having happened before the New Testament Gospels as we know them were written down and circulated. If these miracle stories did indeed circulate in oral tradition before the Gospels appeared in their current form, then by studying the miracle stories we are not simply reading Mark or the other Gospels: it likely that we are actually looking into these old stories for what they convey to us from the oral stage(s) of their transmission.

It is important to note that, as we read and analyze miracle stories in the Gospels, we will not learn how Jesus did his miracles. The Gospels do not tell any procedure by which we modern and postmodern people can perform Jesus's miracles in our twenty-first-century contexts. We must be content to learn what the texts tell us Jesus did, understanding that we cannot perform similar miracles ourselves in our contexts.

Miracle stories in the Synoptic Gospels usually begin with a setting that can be geographical but can also be situational. Jesus did healing miracles for those who were sick or infirm, and Jesus did miracles of provision for those hearers of his who were hungry. Jesus also did miracles in which he showed his power over the forces of nature. After the setting of the miracle is stated, there is often a dialogue between Jesus and another person or persons. Sometimes Jesus's interlocutor is the person who needs healing; sometimes it is one or more demons; sometimes it is the apostles; and sometimes dialogue happens between Jesus or his disciples and loved ones of the person needing to be healed. This dialogue gives readers more information about the particulars of the need for the miracle that Jesus is about to perform. Miracles are often preceded or accompanied by gestures from Jesus or words Jesus speaks; the Gospel According to Mark seems to be fond of Aramaic words. The miraculous act then takes place. After that, readers are told of proof that the miracle really did happen. Often after the proof of the miracle is told, which is evidence that people saw that what Jesus did was effective, there is more material about the reaction of the bystanders to the miraculous occurrence. The grouping of these elements, in this order, constitutes the "form" of miracle stories.

Those who examine Bultmann's *Synoptic Tradition* carefully with respect to miracle stories will discover that the parallels he presented to the miracle stories in Matthew, Mark, and Luke, are extremely numerous. It is true that there are some parallels to the transformation of oral stories into written stories in folktales, but these parallels are overshadowed by miracle

Christobiography, 449–51, as well as Metts, "Neglected Discontinuity," 68–88, along with the literature to which Metts refers.

stories in Jewish, classical, and especially Hellenistic Greek writings, including in some magical texts. There is hardly a detail or characteristic feature of New Testament miracle stories that is not paralleled by analogous details and features of miracle stories in other Hellenistic writings.[4]

What may be more important than the written form of the miracle story in the New Testament is the fact that many if not most of the written miracle stories in the Gospels seem likely to have originated as oral miracle stories. This is probably the best explanation for the pervasive occurrences of miracle stories in several different groupings of literature. If in fact they were originally oral stories, it seems likely that they would have originated as stories told not long after the death and resurrection of Jesus, before the perceived need to create what would later be known as gospels. These oral stories likely originated from some of the memories of those who were alive and who witnessed deeds of power that Jesus performed. I am persuaded that we can date the Gospel According to Mark, around 70 CE, probably after 70 CE,[5] yet the individual stories written in the Gospels are likely from sources that go back earlier in the first century. Hence, if miracle stories existed in forms earlier than the final form of Mark that we now have, this means that they are closer, perhaps decades closer, to Jesus than the Gospel According to Mark itself is.

From my perspective as a Christian, a priest, and a New Testament scholar, it matters very greatly what Jesus did in his earthly life. So for me, and I believe for many readers, historical questions about Jesus are very appropriate to ask and to attempt to answer. I would like to know what Jesus did during his earthly life. I would like to know what Jesus did and thought he was doing at the Last Supper, and after the Last Supper. I would like to know how frequent Jesus's resurrection appearances were. I believe that many of the readers of this book also would like to know the answers to these and other historical questions.

After decades of study and teaching, I believe that if Jesus did not perform miracles, then there are writings and groups of writings by early Jesus-believers that defy reasonable explanation. These writings would include the Gospels and the Acts of the Apostles. Thus, as I examine the various miracle stories in Mark, I want to discern what is historical in these stories. Ultimately, I want to look through these miracle stories in Mark so

---

4. Bultmann, *Synoptic Tradition*, 218–44.

5. For an argument in favor of a much earlier dating of Mark, see Bernier, *Rethinking*, 69–77.

that I can understand as clearly as possible what Jesus actually did, and how what he did was believed in and taught in the first-century church. Given that the Gospels of the New Testament were written close in time to the life of Jesus, especially in comparison with other writings from antiquity, the Gospels deserve quite a bit of credence as historical sources. This book is an effort to help readers make their way through the earliest of the Gospels.

Jesus spoke a dialect of Aramaic that others spoke and understood in Israel in the first century CE, and so it stands to reason that his sayings were in the Aramaic language. To the extent that they were remembered by Jesus's earliest followers, they would have been remembered first in Aramaic. At some point in the first century of our era, there was a desire to bring the remembered sayings of Jesus from Aramaic to Greek. The production of the sources of the Gospels as we know them took place. After some years or perhaps several decades, the earliest of the Gospels we have in the New Testament was produced. This is the book we know as the Gospel According to Mark.

The Gospel According to Mark at first had only its first verse as a title: "The beginning of the Gospel of Jesus Christ," to which may have been added "the Son of God." There is much to be said about the Gospel According to Mark, which is its traditional title. If Mark was the earliest of the three Synoptic Gospels (Matthew, Mark, and Luke), then Mark was a written source for the Gospels of Matthew and Luke. And if in fact Mark was a source for Matthew and Luke, this is a great testament to the trust that the authors, compilers, or editors of Matthew and Luke had in the basic structure of Mark. The writers of Matthew and Luke used Mark as the skeleton or framework for their Gospels. The writers of Matthew and Luke did not generally agree with Mark's low estimation of the apostles. They added material they thought Mark was lacking, such as stories of the birth and infancy of Jesus, together with appearances of the resurrected Jesus and a large amount of material that relates the teaching of Jesus. It is very notable that Matthew's birth and infancy story (Matt 1:1—2:23) is different from Luke's (Luke 1:1—2:52), so they did not get them from a common source. The same is true for the narratives of Jesus's resurrection appearances, which Mark 16:1–8 lacks.

Early believers in Jesus believed that in the life of Jesus, God was making an intervention into the world of humanity. God, whom Jesus addressed as Father, was not a God who was far off or who would never have anything to do with humankind. The merciful and loving God whom Jesus addressed as Father was a God who chose to intervene and enter the human world in order to save it.

Miracles are examples of the loving nature of God the Father. The stories of Jesus's miracles were preserved in oral form through retelling, and they were preserved in written form, perhaps first in "chains" (catenae) or collections of miracle stories and eventually in the Gospels we know.[6] They not only illustrate the loving nature of God: they also illustrate the power of Jesus during his earthly, preresurrection life. I believe that miracle stories also contribute to the images of the apostles: they convey to the Gospel readers healings and other events that the first followers of Jesus saw and experienced. Thus, if one were to ask why the apostles were important, an answer could be that they saw what Jesus did, in addition to hearing what Jesus taught, during his earthly life. Apostles, however, did not just see miracles being done; they also gave the rest of their lives to the work of spreading faith in Jesus to countless people in many places and cultures. So the stories of Jesus's miracles also gave further believability to the preaching of the apostles.

Further Healings

Miracle stories are grouped into three types: healing miracles, miracles of provision, and nature miracles. In the rest of this section of Mark (1:16—3:6), the miracle stories are narratives of healings by Jesus. Healing miracles are also scattered elsewhere in Mark. By my count there are sixteen healing miracles in Mark, out of a total of twenty-four "deeds of power."

The healing of Simon's mother-in-law in 1:29–31 is an abbreviated miracle story. It does have, briefly, the form of a miracle story: the (temporal) setting of the healing, the dialogue of her relatives with Jesus, the gesture of healing, and the literary proof of the miracle. The healing of many persons at evening (1:32–34) is even more abbreviated; the only interesting feature is the final phrase: "he would not permit the demons to speak, because they knew him" (1:34). The contrast is between the demons, who know full well who and what Jesus is, versus the apostles, who definitely do not know, and who will not know until Peter confesses his faith in Jesus as Son of God in 8:27–30.

Even in the midst of many miracle stories there are interspersed reports of Jesus's praying and teaching (1:35–39). A further miracle story is

6. Achtemeier, "Toward the Isolation"; and Achtemeier, "Origin and Function."

the healing of a man who had leprosy (1:40–45). The emphasis in this story is on Jesus's interaction with the man with leprosy, in which Jesus emphasizes his own wish that the man be cleansed of his skin disease (1:40–41). The proof of the miracle's effectiveness is given in two ways: by the simple statement of his healing and also by the fact that Jesus sent him to the priest to certify his healing. Though Jesus commands him to be silent about his healing (1:43–44), the man tells about his healing freely, so that Jesus becomes so famous that he cannot stay in the city but has to stay out of sight in the country; yet even then "people came to him from every quarter" (1:45), although Mark's readers are not told how people learned of Jesus's healing miracles.

The healing of the paralyzed man in 2:1–12 is a dramatic story. Jesus is in Capernaum again (2:1). Four men are carrying a paralyzed man. Jesus is so popular that these men cannot get in to see him, so they take the paralyzed man up on the roof, and then bore an opening through the roof and let the paralyzed man down on his mat. Jesus not only heals the paralyzed man; before the healing, he also forgives his sins (2:5–9), which has even further implications for what Jesus has authority to do. In 2:10 Jesus tells the gathered assembly that the "Son of Man," meaning Jesus himself, "has authority on earth to forgive sins." Thus, the text of Mark is filled with hints and specific sayings that tell readers that Jesus has a special, unique status with respect to God. This saying about the Son of Man having authority on earth is a follow-up to God the Father's saying to Jesus, "You are my Son, the Beloved; with you I am well pleased" (1:11), which took place immediately after "the Spirit" was seen "descending like a dove on him" (1:10). In this way, we can clearly recognize that miracle stories, in addition to narrating events that happened in Jesus's lifetime, also are deeply christological. They ensure that readers know who Jesus truly is, in sharp contrast to the disciples, who, despite being in the actual physical presence of Jesus, do not come to know him until the Peter's confession in 8:27–30.

A More Controversial Apostle Is Called (2:13–17)

Jesus had already taken pains to heal some outcasts, namely, the person who had a demon in the synagogue in Capernaum (1:23–28) as well as the man with leprosy (1:40–45). These were people who were religious outcasts. The more conventional Jewish people did not want to get near them. Their alienation from the more respectable Jews was because of their having a demon or having an infectious skin disease. People who were ritually clean did not want to get the demon or the skin disease that the unclean had. Thus keeping a distance was a matter of self-defense for both the sick and the well, and the motive across the divide was self-preservation: the afflicted men were not welcome in the more respectable Jewish circles

Levi the tax collector, however, was an outcast for a different reason. As a tax collector, Levi collected taxes to support the Roman occupation government in Israel. He was actually a collaborator with the Roman oppressors of Jews in Israel. After Jesus asked Levi to become one of his followers, Jesus and his followers (who were now numerous, 2:15) were invited to eat dinner in Levi's house. What was worse was the fact that there were also "many tax collectors and sinners" along with Levi in his house. Readers are not told what sins the "sinners" had committed or were committing. Yet the scandal that arose around Jesus and his group attracted the attention with "the scribes of the Pharisees" (or "the scribes and the Pharisees," 2:16), so that they questioned Jesus's followers, who are now called disciples, asking, "Why does he eat with tax collectors and sinners?" Jesus heard their interrogation of his disciples. Notably, he did not disagree with this evaluation of some of the other dinner guests as sinners. Yet he defends his decision to associate with them and even eat with them (2:17). Once again Jesus appears to prefer associating with outcasts rather than respectable people: "I have come not to call the righteous but sinners" (2:15). So, Mark tells readers that Jesus's decision to be with and to help outcasts and even to call an outcast to be one of his disciples was very much part of his understanding of his mission. The close followers of Jesus were among the ones who most needed Jesus's mission of calling, healing, and teaching. Far from being shining, positive examples of righteousness or learning, the followers of Jesus are not among the respectable Jews whom Jesus encountered. The Gospel According to Mark makes crystal clear that neither Jesus's disciples nor the people Jesus healed nor those with whom Jesus is willing to eat are high on any known scale of social respectability or honor. In fact, what Jesus was doing, according to Mark, was nothing less than radically overturning the conventional system of honor and shame.[7] As we continue to read Mark, we will see more and more of this.

---

7. Robert Jewett in his *Romans: A Commentary*, 48–53, argued that Paul in his Letter to the Romans "criticizes and reverses the official system of honor achieved through piety on which the empire after Augustus rested" (48).

Reversal in the Age to Come (2:18–22)

One of the most important characteristics of the teachings of Jesus was the belief that the ways all sorts of matters are ordered in the present life will be reversed in the life to come. There is a technical term for this: eschatological reversal. The word "eschatological" refers to the end of time, when there will be a divine intervention in history. The saying, "the first shall be last, and the last shall be first" (Mark 10:31; Matt 19:30; compare with Luke 13:30 and Matt 20:16), is an excellent illustration of this reversal in the age to come.

The well-known saying in Mark 2:21–22 about putting new wine in old wineskins also suggests that there is a conflict between what is old and what is new. If one puts new wine in old wineskins, the fermentation of the new wine will cause the old wineskins to burst. This saying suggests, in its unique way, that even though Jesus stands strongly within the traditions of Judaism, especially its scriptures, Jesus's ministry—which the apostles will share and eventually take up themselves—will cause conflicts with certain traditions of Jewish life and belief. During the earthly lifetime of Jesus, the new wine of Jesus's ministry had not yet burst the old wineskins; Jesus's ministry was a renewal movement within Judaism. Yet readers like us in the twenty-first century may well observe that the ministry of Jesus did in fact do what the saying about the burst wineskins implies. Like all religions, Judaism continued to be practiced and thus continued to develop. Yet while John the Baptizer and Jesus were prophets within Judaism, they were quite critical of some practices by some Jews. They did not get along with "the scribes and Pharisees." John and Jesus were both within Judaism and critical of it.[8] Their criticism of how some Jews practiced their religion did not sit well with the Jerusalem hierarchy of Judaism. What Jesus was doing, and what John the Baptizer had done, constituted new wine in the old wineskins of Jewish practice. To some extent, the beliefs and practices of the Essenes, who wrote and preserved the Dead Sea Scrolls at Qumran, also introduced new wine into the older wineskins of Judaism.

---

8. To quote J.-P. Vernant in his *Problèms de la guerre*, 21: "There is rivalry only between those who resemble each other, who recognize the same values, judge themselves by the same criteria, agree to play the same game." The quotation and its translation are from Nicole Loraux, *Invention*, 383n83.

Working on the Sabbath (2:23–28)

In Mark 2:5–9, Jesus had already done something that deeply displeased some of his hearers: he forgave sins. The forgiveness of sins was something that God was able to do, not human beings, according to the scriptures and traditions of Judaism. Even more intriguing, this forgiveness of sins was connected—somehow—with the healing of the paralyzed man in 2:1–12. The healing of the paralyzed man and the forgiveness of his sins were acts which suggested either the activity or the permission of God—or both. To forgive sins using the divine passive as Jesus did ("Son, your sins are forgiven") implies that one (in this case Jesus) speaks for God. Even Jesus's addressing the man as "son" may suggest Jesus's special relationship with God.

In this passage, 2:23–28, Jesus allowed his disciples to pluck grain in grainfields on the Sabbath. This act was seen by the Pharisees as work on the Sabbath (2:24), which was a violation of the commandment against working on the Sabbath (Exod 20:8–10; Deut 5:12–15). Jesus counters their interpretation of the Torah with the illustration of David and his soldiers eating the bread of the presence in 1 Sam 21:1–6. The incident in 1 Sam 21 presupposed that David and the soldiers under his command were hungry, which was also true of Jesus and his disciples. Hence, Jesus's allowing his disciples to pluck heads of grain on the Sabbath had scriptural precedent in the incident when David ordered Ahimelech to give him and his soldiers the bread of the presence, and Ahimelech complied. An obvious justification for Jesus's allowing his disciples to pick grain on the Sabbath was that by picking and eating the grain, the disciples would no longer be hungry and could continue to accompany Jesus on his journeys. Thus for Jesus in Mark's Gospel, picking grain on the Sabbath was work done for the purpose of preserving the lives of his disciples. The preservation of life could be seen as a legitimate reason to get around even as important a legal provision as the fourth of the Ten Commandments. Of course, this text does not portray Jesus as being somehow anti-Jewish; rather, it shows him entering as a fellow Jew into a Jewish debate.

Healing on the Sabbath (3:1–6)

The final story in this section of Mark portrays Jesus once more as an apparent violator of the fourth commandment, which forbade people to work on the Sabbath day, which began on Friday evening and extended until

Saturday evening. To alert readers to the meaning and importance of this story, Mark 3:2 is extremely direct: "They were observing [Jesus] to see whether he would cure him on the Sabbath, so that they might accuse him." As we can read in 3:6, this is exactly what happened. Jesus did cure the man with the withered hand, and the healing was on the Sabbath. Thus, between vv. 2 and 6 of Mark chapter 3, two factors are stated: the justification for Jesus's healing on the Sabbath (3:4–5a), and the performance of the miracle (3:3, 5b). Readers can clearly see the familiar form of gospel miracle stories: the setting and situation of the healing (3:1–2), the dialogue with the person needing healing and with bystanders (3:3–4), the performance of the miracle (3:5a), the proof that the miracle was effective (3:5b), and the reaction to the miracle by others (3:6). Yet the focus of this miracle story is not so much on the effectiveness of the miracle performed by Jesus but on Jesus's intentional healing of the man on the Sabbath. And the reaction to the miracle is not a positive amazement from the crowd; nor is it an increased desire from the people for Jesus's healing ministry, as we have read elsewhere in Markan miracle stories: the reaction is against the propriety of the healing, because Jesus performed it on the Sabbath. This reaction evidently portrays "the Pharisees" as those who favor the strict observance of the prohibition of work on the Sabbath over the mercy shown by Jesus in doing the healing. Joel Marcus points out that Jesus as "the holy one of God" favors "the apocalyptic destruction of demons and disease," so that his healing of the man with the withered hand "is a fulfillment rather than an infraction" of the fourth commandment.[9] The Pharisees of Mark 3:1–6, however, see Jesus as a violator of the commandment, so they are portrayed as legalists. Yet Mark 3:6 actually shifts the focus away from their legalism per se and moves it towards the political decision by Pharisees as well as Herodians to plot with each other "how they would destroy him."

So this miracle story in 3:1–6 is much more than a miracle story. It has the form of a miracle story, to be sure, yet the story as a whole focuses, neither on the power of Jesus to heal the man with the withered hand, nor on the propriety of Jesus's healing him on the Sabbath. The major upshot of the story is that this is the first major notice by Mark of Jesus's incurring an organized opposition. Even when Jesus does his exorcism in the synagogue in Capernaum in 1:21–28, the crowd reaction in 1:27–28 is unquestionably positive, so that "his fame began to spread throughout the surrounding region of Galilee" (1:28). This positive crowd reaction continued during the

---

9. Marcus, *Mark 1–8*, 252–53.

healings at evening in 1:32–34 and during the healing of a leper in 1:40–45. Yet even as Jesus was doing the good deeds by performing his healings in that region of Galilee, it was beginning to get dangerous for him, "so that Jesus could no longer go into a town openly, but stayed out in the country; and people came to him from every quarter" (1:45). The positive public impact seen in 1:45—2:2, which was his celebrity due to his power to heal, turned in 3:1–2 to his being watched in the Capernaum synagogue, and then escalated in 3:6 to two groups of opponents actually plotting his death.

Conclusion

The dramatic change in the public reaction to Jesus's healing miracles is very significant. Instead of the public and highly positive reaction of people to Jesus, in 3:6 the reaction brings about a private meeting between two particular groups of people within the Jewish community—groups still in Galilee, not yet in Jerusalem. This meeting was held to plot Jesus's death. As we continue to read in Mark, this organized opposition to Jesus will increase in numbers and power. We will continue to read miracle stories; some of them will be more typical, and others less typical. As we continue to read Mark, we will also read parables, which are stories that illustrate points Jesus was teaching his disciples. All in all, we will read of an increasing level of conflict between Jesus and others outside his circle of disciples and hearers. This conflict will result in Jesus's suffering and death.

4

Further Ministry in Galilee
Mark 3:7—4:34

THIS SECTION OF MARK continues the portrayal of Jesus's ministry in Galilee, the region in which he grew up, in the north of Israel. In Mark's narrative in 3:7–12 we encounter a summary of Jesus's healing ministry, the healing of multitudes by the sea. We will also read several parables. Jesus's teaching by parables was an important and apparently distinctive part of his ministry as a teacher.

Healing Crowds by the Sea (3:7–12)

This passage in Mark is a summary of Jesus's healing ministry, rather than a narrative of a particular healing miracle. Mark 3:7–10 gives readers the situation of Jesus as he had departed from Capernaum via the Sea of Galilee. His popularity was such that Jesus evidently feared that the crowds from many different places would crush him, because of their desire to get near him, in order to be cured of their diseases. The disciples were told previously to have a boat ready for Jesus to escape from the crush of the crowds (3:9–10). The next couple of verses describe encounters with "unclean spirits": when they saw Jesus, they fell down in worship before him and loudly proclaimed that he is Son of God (3:11), to which Jesus responded by ordering them to be silent (3:12) but, very notably, not by contradicting what they said about him. Whatever one may make of the demons, the Gospel of Mark is once again telling its readers the Christology that that author favors. According to Mark, Jesus is Son of God during his earthly life beginning at his baptism, when God the Father addressed him, saying, "You are my Son, the Beloved" (1:11). Miracle stories are deeply christological, and this summary of Jesus's miracles likewise alerts readers once again of Jesus's identity as the Messiah. In this verse, as in others, the readers of Mark are enabled to know what the demons knew and what the apostles did not know at this point.

Jesus's Selection of the Twelve (3:13-19)

Careful readers of the New Testament Gospels will encounter different titles for the closest followers of Jesus. For Mark, a favored title for these people is "the Twelve."[1] Matthew's favored title is "disciples," which is intimately connected with Matthew's strong emphasis on Jesus's role in that gospel as a teacher.[2] The Gospel According to Luke uses both the titles "disciples" and "apostles." In Luke 10:1-12 there is the sending of the seventy (or seventy-two) and their return to Jesus (10:17-20), yet in these passages Luke avoids the term "disciples" as well as "apostles." Since it is quite likely that Matthew and Luke were written in their present form in the late first century CE, using Mark as a written source, by the time Matthew and Luke were written, almost all the original followers of Jesus had died.[3]

---

1. Mark's use of "the twelve," far from being a neutral term, probably has a symbolic meaning. Joel Marcus in *Mark 1-8* points out the links between the number twelve and "the twelve tribes of Israel and therefore with the concept of the eschatological fullness of the people of God" (411; see also especially his discussion of "twelve" on 514-15). Marcus stresses the insight that the use of the number twelve for the disciples suggests "eschatological completion" (514). Adela Yarbro Collins in *Mark* argues at greater length that both Mark 3:13-19 and the Temple Scroll in Cave 11 at Qumran "must be seen in the context of the expectation of the restoration of the twelve tribes of Israel in the last days" (216), so that "[i]t is likely that the historical Jesus chose twelve special associates in order to symbolize the restoration of the twelve tribes of Israel that was about to take place" (217).

2. The Greek word *mathētai*, usually translated by the English word "disciples," means "students" since the verb *manthanein* means "to teach."

3. By the time the Pastoral Epistles (1 Timothy, 2 Timothy, and Titus) were written, probably in the late first century or early second century CE, most of the first apostles, including Paul himself, had died. This is the reason that the authority structure in local congregations in 1 Timothy and Titus no longer included apostles. On the role of apostles, see the recent study by Alastair Stewart, *Original Bishops*, as well as Kertelge, *Gemeinde und Amt im Neuen Testament*, 102-28.

The meaning of the term "apostles" (*apostoloi*) was in the process of changing at the time Mark was composed. This was just before the time as the other Gospels were being written and edited in the first century of our era. This fact is reflected in significant disagreement in the Greek and Latin manuscripts of the text of Mark 3:14, where some of them add "whom he also named apostles." Some of the sources in early Christian literature assume that an *apostolos* was strictly one of the twelve direct followers of Jesus (see a notable example in Acts 1:21–22). This is the view that we can read in the Gospels, as opposed to the understanding of *apostoloi* in the Letters of the Pauline corpus.[4] In the Letters of Paul, an *apostolos* was any Christian who was called and commissioned by the risen Christ, including Paul himself and including people such as Andronicus and apparently his wife, Junia (Rom 16:7). In Rom 16:1-2, Phoebe is a *diakonos*, which is the identical term that Paul uses for himself and Apollos in 1 Cor 3:5, although elsewhere both are called apostles. It is clear that different groups of people in the early church undertook different practices and had different understandings of ministries and the authority of ministers in the church. In the case of the Pauline corpus as written in the first century and possibly in the second, and as edited in the second century, it is not hard for us to see that changes in understandings of the church and its patterns of leadership were in progress.

Jesus Is Thought to Be Crazy (3:20–21)[5]

The writer of Mark seems to have a basically negative view of Jesus's family. As they are portrayed in Mark, the family of Jesus thought he was out of

---

4. The word *apostolos* is used only once in Matthew. In Mark, in addition to the variant reading in 3:14, it is used only in 6:30. It is used six times in Luke, but twenty-eight times in Acts, and thirty-four times in the Pauline corpus.

5. Following the Nestle-Aland 28th edition (2012) of the Greek text, as well as the 27th edition (1992) and the 26th edition (1979), I am including "then he went home" as part of 3:20. The New Revised Standard Version Updated Edition (NRSVue, 2021) and the United Bible Societies' *The Greek New Testament*, 5th rev. ed. (2014) also follow Nestle-Aland on this point; this was a change from the New Revised Standard Version of 1989, the Revised Standard Version of 1952, and the King James Version of 1611. Fischer et al., *Biblia Sacra iuxta Vulgatam Versionem*, 4th ed. (1994) had also included these words as part of 3:20. So do *The Greek New Testament* produced at Tyndale House, Cambridge (2017); and the *Gospel According to Mark* in *Novum Testamentum Graecum: editio critica maior*, 1.2/1 (2021); along with Holmes, *Greek New Testament: SBL Edition* (2010); and Huck and Greeven, *Synopsis of the First Three Gospels* (1981).

his mind, and on this point they were in agreement with "the scribes who came down from Jerusalem" (3:22), and with "the crowd" who said that Jesus "has gone out of his mind" (3:21). Thus, the family of Jesus "went out to restrain him" (3:21). Mark's negative treatment of the family of Jesus is fully consistent with its treatment of the apostles.

Collusion with Satan? / The Sin Against the Holy Spirit (3:22–30)

While the family of Jesus had heard the reports of Jesus's unusual behavior, reports that he was believed to be mentally ill (3:21), the scribes who came from Jerusalem to investigate Jesus gave their more negative judgment in 3:22: Jesus's behavior was due to his being possessed by Beelzebul. The reasoning for their judgment, which would have made sense to many people in the ancient world, was that Jesus had the power to cast out demons because he had a stronger demon. Since demons were the cause of illnesses and infirmities when Jesus lived on earth, when he healed the sick, he did so by casting out the demons the sick people had. Yet Jesus turns this charge against him on its head: if Jesus is casting out demons by means of Satan, as his enemies argue, what this really means is that Satan's power is coming to an end (3:26). Thus the coming of Jesus was not the occasion for him to collude with Satan, as Jesus's opponents charged, but actually to combat the power of Satan.

The Family of Jesus (3:31–35)

Surprisingly, the family of Jesus does not understand or agree with Jesus's mission and ministry. Apparently they had heard the scuttlebutt that Jesus "has gone out of his mind" (3:21) so that "they went out to restrain him." They were either concerned about their family's reputation or about Jesus's well-being, if not both. Yet for them to "restrain" Jesus would have been to stop him from doing his ministry of preaching and healing, so their seeking to restrain Jesus indicates their disapproval of his mission. By 3:31, the mother and brothers of Jesus are outside where he is preaching, and they are calling for him to come outside and so to cease his public ministry at that time. Jesus not only refuses to do so; he says something far more radical: the true mother and brothers of Jesus are not his blood relatives, but "whoever does the will of God is my brother and sister and mother" (3:35).

Thus, as Jesus teaches, his true family is the group of people that follow him rather than those to whom he is related by blood. This observation was not simply a historical comment about Jesus's family, but also a comment about the closeness of the ongoing community of Jesus-believers to Jesus himself.

Parables

The fact that Jesus taught in parables is the best-known aspect of Jesus's teaching ministry. Parables were stories that compared various phenomena with each other, and it is now generally believed that parables were told to illustrate or teach a very few points, perhaps only one point. Centuries ago, scholars analyzed Jesus's parables with the assumption that they were primarily allegorical. Later, drawing on the justly famous work of Adolf Jülicher,[6] scholars came to believe that Jesus's parables contained no allegory.

The famous parables grouped in chapter 4 of Mark are about the kingdom of God. Several are based on ideas about growing things, such as plants or trees, in comparison with the growth of the kingdom of God as the result of the preaching of the word of God. Preaching God's word is something that prophets did and that Jesus also did, and it is also what the disciples of Jesus would do as their major ministry after the death and resurrection of Jesus. Thus, the comments Mark makes on the growth of the kingdom of God must be considered to be not just about Jesus's preaching and teaching ministry, but about the ministry of the apostles and other teachers and preachers after Jesus's resurrection. When followers of Jesus preached and taught the message of Jesus, the kingdom grew and the church attracted followers.

The Parable of the Sower (4:1–9) and the Meaning of Parables (4:10–20)

This section is introduced by 4:1–2. Jesus was not teaching on land; he was in a boat (cf. 3:9). There is a summary (4:2) of what will follow in 4:3–20: "he taught them many things in parables." The parabolic nature of 4:3–10 is clear. Just as a person who sowed his seeds rather too widely would do, the sower in this parable throws the seeds on several different kinds of soil, and in most of those soils—on the footpaths, on the rocky ground, and in places

---

6. Jülicher, *Gleichnisreden Jesu*.

with many thorny plants—healthy plants could not grow from the seeds sown by the sower. This parable is about evangelism, and in most of the cases of where the seeds are sown, there will be none of the desired results of agriculture; there will only be a waste of seeds thrown haphazardly by the sower. Yet this parable does not seem to advise a more careful way of sowing seeds; this parable tells readers that even when evangelism is done faithfully and even effectively, not everybody who hears the word of the Lord will respond favorably to it. This is not because of the quality of the seeds—the word of God—but because there will be many times when the "soils"—the hearers of the word of God—will not choose to receive it and respond to it favorably. In those "soils" that will respond favorably to the seeds sown, the yield of "grain" will be "thirtyfold and sixtyfold and a hundredfold." This parable contains surprise: Even though the seed is excellent, there will be many places where even though the seeds germinate, they cannot grow, because they are walked on, or because they fall where there is no depth of soil, or because they must compete with aggressive vegetation that will be deadly to the plants that the seedlings might have become.

This parable uses simple ideas about agriculture as a way to deal with evangelism and its many problems. It provides practical advice for the later first-century readers of Mark—wisdom that the results of evangelism will likely never be 100 percent. There will be difficulties in the proclamation of the word of God: people who "hear the word and immediately receive it with joy," but subsequently fall away from the Jesus-community. Others receive the word, but other things in their lives, namely, "the cares of the world and the delight in riches" will "choke" the word (4:19). So even though evangelism and other ministries might be done in good ways, there will be people who never really receive the word at all, as well as those who receive the word and subsequently fall away from faith in Jesus and participation in the Jesus-community. This is good advice for those involved in ministry, both now and in the first century. Those who would reject this advice from the Gospel of Mark would suffer greatly from discouragement, not only from persecution but also from people who may identify with the Jesus-community for a time but will not be truly receptive to the word of God and thus not fruitful in ministry in the long term.

In 4:10–12 there is a separate parable that itself deals with the issue of why Jesus teaches using parables, which is an integral part of the issue of what the parables meant, as far as Mark was telling the readers. The Twelve, being actual hearers of Jesus, have enjoyed a great advantage over the readers of Mark. It was to the Twelve that "the secret of the kingdom of God" was imparted, and yet, as the readers of Mark will come to learn, it is the Twelve who mismanage the secret. They are given the keys to unlock the meanings of parables by Jesus their teacher. Those who did not hear the actual words of Jesus during his earthly life, or who do not read the Gospel According to Mark, may not gain the full understanding of the teachings of Jesus: for them it will be only "parables" or "riddles," so that 4:11 should be translated as follows: "And he said to them, 'To you is imparted the mystery of the kingdom of God; to those others outside, everything is riddles.'" In Mark, parables that the hearers do not understand are the same as riddles: words are used, but the meaning of the words Jesus speaks is far from clear. So there is a dichotomy between the idea that the Twelve are supposed to understand Jesus's parables, and the actual fact that the Twelve do not. If they understand anything of Jesus's teaching in parables, it is because Jesus explains the parables to them privately (4:34).

Parables of the Kingdom (4:21–32)

Mark 4:21–25 may be a collection of two or more sayings. The parable of the lamp in 4:21–23 is both about evangelism and about reversal in the age to come. It is desirable that the word of God be fully proclaimed, rather than hidden under a basket or a bed. In 4:21–22, these two sayings are connected through their content: they include matter about a lamp and the proper use of a lamp, to give light. In 4:21, the contrast is between the ability of a lamp properly or improperly placed to give light. In 4:22, there is a different contrast, which is laid over the contrast in 4:21: the contrast in 4:22 is between matters kept secret now and made fully visible in the future, when the kingdom of God fully comes. Mark 4:23 is an exhortation to listen: "If a person has ears to hear, let that person hear!" (my trans.). Since various things are hidden in the present age, as Jesus teaches in Mark 4:21–23, people will be made fully aware of them when the kingdom fully comes. Because of the presence of the Gospel According to Mark in the present age, readers of Mark who "have ears to hear" (4:23) are informed about Jesus and the kingdom of God. The writer of Mark appears to believe that not everybody has "ears to hear," especially in light of the parable of the sower (4:1–9), which concludes in v. 9 with the same exhortation to those who "have ears to hear," which is a wake-up call to the readers of Mark.

Mark 4:26–29 is the parable of the seed growing secretly. It does not have a parallel in Luke and only a very incomplete parallel in Matt 13:24–30. It seems that this parable appears here in Mark 4 simply because it deals with seeds and sowing. The seed, having been sown (meaning the word of God having been proclaimed), can sprout and grow without any subsequent effort on the part of the sower of the seeds—without the original preacher of the kingdom doing any other ministry later. This parable actually appears strongly to have come from the historical Jesus, since later generations of the church would hardly want to suggest that the results of ministry are not due to hard, patient work.[7] Yet this parable which says that the word of God can propagate secretly is a way of talking about the strong and prolific growth of the kingdom of God, sometimes without any effort on the part of ministers of the gospel other than initially "sowing the seeds," namely, proclaiming the word of God, presumably in the proper place, at the proper time, and in the proper way. Before the sower knows it, or even if the sower never knows it, the seed will have produced "first the blade, then the ear, then the full grain in the ear" (4:28). This means that when the kingdom of God grows, it really grows quickly and strongly.

In Mark 4:30–32, the famous parable of the mustard seed, the smallness of the mustard seed is contrasted with the luxuriant growth of the mustard shrub. This suggests that even though the mustard seed starts out very small, its growth is quite surprising and strong. This symbolizes the kingdom of God. The number of people that the church includes starts out small and yet in a surprisingly short time becomes large.

Why Did Jesus Use Parables? (4:33–34)

The final verses of this section, 4:33–34, suggest to readers that, in addition to the parables reproduced here in Mark 4, there were many other parables of Jesus in circulation through oral tradition, if they were not also written in various texts about which the writer of Mark knew. Much has been written about parables by New Testament scholars, and there is nothing to suggest a clear demarcation between texts that did come from the historical Jesus and those that came from the early church. In an important sense, all of these parables came through the early church in the three and a half decades from Jesus's death and resurrection in about 33 CE until the

---

7. See, for example, Paul's statements about his hard work in 1 Thess 2:9; 1 Corinthians 3:6–15; 4:12; and 2 Cor 6:4–5; in the Pauline tradition see also 2 Tim 4:6–7.

writing of Mark's Gospel in about 70 CE. We have no doubt whatsoever that they came through the teaching activities of communities of early Jesus-followers. The only question is the extent to which we can reasonably identify the origin of several of these sayings in Jesus himself. The efforts by form critics, most notably Martin Dibelius and Rudolf Bultmann, to identify Jesus as the originator of many sayings in the Gospels were numerous. These efforts have very often been misunderstood, as if scholars like Dibelius and Bultmann were somehow unchristian and complete skeptics about knowing anything at all of Jesus. While many people disagree with the conclusions of the classic form critics, their work raised historical questions about Jesus, his teaching, and the relationships between his words and deeds, on the one hand, and the written Gospels we now possess, on the other. These historical and literary questions are legitimate and reasonable. They also have not gone away.

5

Miracles, Rejection, and Murder
Mark 4:35—6:56

THIS SECTION OF MARK includes a great number of miracles, and yet the miraculous is interrupted by the murder of John the Baptizer at the order of Herod Antipas in 6:17–29.[1] This section also includes Jesus's being rejected in "his hometown"[2] (6:1–6a) and his inability to do many deeds of power there. Perhaps this painful rejection in Nazareth, where he might have been very well received, is a reason that Jesus then sent the Twelve out "two by two" (6:6b–13) for ministries that included exorcisms in villages in Galilee other than Nazareth. The most spectacular exorcism in the whole New Testament, by far, is the exorcism of the demoniac in 5:1–20 in "the country of the Gerasenes," and this notable name for those people who lived in Gerasa may actually have been Gadarenes or Gergesenes, depending on which one is the original reading in 5:1. Less spectacular to the readers of Mark are the stories of Jesus's stilling storms on the sea in 4:35–41 and 6:45–52. All in all, this section of Mark is filled with miracle stories of various kinds: healings, exorcisms, a healing miracle sandwiched in the middle of another healing miracle, topped off by the famous miracle of the provision of food for five thousand people (6:30–44) and a concluding summary of healing miracles (6:53–56).

---

1. I use the term "murder" because his death, according to Mark, was not the result of any legal proceeding but was due to the whims of Herod and his wife Herodias.

2. Nazareth is only mentioned by name once in Mark, at 1:9.

Miracles, Rejection, and Murder

The Stilling of the Storm (4:35–41)

In this story, the usual elements of miracle stories are prominent. The setting of the miracle is Jesus's desire to go to the other side of the Sea of Galilee. Taking leave of the crowd allowed Jesus more time to be alone with his disciples, which is consistent with 4:34 where "he explained everything privately to his disciples." Yet 4:35–36 marks not only a geographical and thus situational change for the ministry of Jesus; it also marks a change from material in this gospel, which is mostly the teaching of the people by means of parables, to material that is mostly Jesus's doing deeds of power, namely, miracles. This section opens not with a healing miracle but with a nature miracle. In order to get to the other side of the Sea of Galilee, Jesus and his disciples use a boat to make their first sea crossing. This crossing, however, is hampered and made dangerous by a windstorm that was blowing water into the boat. The fact that too much water was coming into the boat made this sea crossing unsafe. The danger for Jesus and his disciples constituted by these details is analogous to the threat to life that serious or chronic disease causes, which we read about in the settings of healing miracles. This danger from the wind and sea causes the disciples to fear for their safety in the boat. The disciples' fear and uncertainty is the reason for the miracle, which was for their benefit. Jesus, who was asleep in the boat, is awakened. His dialogue with the disciples constitutes only their desperate question: "Teacher, do you not care that we are perishing?" (4:38). Jesus performs the miracle by rebuking the wind and giving the order to the sea, "Peace! Be still!" (4:39). Instead of the usual crowd reaction to a healing miracle, we have here the disciples' reaction of "great awe" and their questioning of each other about Jesus, as they ask who Jesus is since he is in control of forces of nature (4:41). Thus Mark allows the final verse of chapter 4 to raise the christological question in the minds of readers about the identity and power of Jesus. Importantly, none of the disciples has confessed that Jesus is the Messiah, as Simon will do in 8:29. Instead of a question that Simon alone will answer in chapter 8, here at 4:41 apparently all the disciples in the boat with Jesus ask the christological question: "Who is this that even the wind and the sea obey him?" The posing of the christological question here provokes the readers of Mark to begin to ask this question in earnest for themselves. In other words, who was this Jewish prophet, who was none other than the Son of God, about whom we have been hearing or reading? A further question is what the readers' belief in Jesus as miracle worker, preacher, teacher, and Son of God, means. So, as we read the story of the stilling of the storm in 4:35–41, many questions are going on behind and in the text of Mark and, as far as the author of Mark hoped, also in the minds of readers.

The Gerasene Demoniac (5:1–20)

The most spectacular encounter between Jesus and demons is the exorcism of the Gerasene demoniac. Here, as in many other places in the Synoptic Gospels, we presuppose Markan priority—that the Gospel According to Mark underlies the Gospels According to Matthew and According to Luke. These latter two Gospels, it is believed, used Mark as a written source. This accounts well for the parallels in Matt 8:28–34 and Luke 8:26–39, in comparison with Mark 5:1–20. Yet their use of Mark did not mean that the editors of Matthew and Luke thought it right to preserve slavishly every detail of the Markan text. Some of the details of how bizarre the Gerasene demoniac's behavior was were indeed too graphic for Matthew and Luke; these writers edited many of the specifics out of their reiterations of this miracle story in the other two Synoptic Gospels.

In his well-known work on the Acts of the Apostles, the late Richard I. Pervo showed that many of the episodes in the Acts of the Apostles, like episodes in Hellenistic popular literature, were written so that they had literary entertainment value.[3] Mark 5:1–20 is as unforgettable a scene as any in the Gospels. What is so striking in this passage is the behavior of the man afflicted by the demon (or more precisely, demons). The bizarre character of his behavior while inhabited by multiple demons tells readers in very graphic terms just how deeply in need of an exorcism this man truly was. The first readers of Mark could surely affirm how terrible the demoniac's afflictions were, especially since he had not one but apparently thousands of demons, given that his name was Legion (5:9) and that a Roman legion would have comprised some five thousand soldiers. The profoundly afflicted man speaks mostly in the first person plural because he is inhabited by so many unclean spirits (5:3–5). The extraordinary nature of the man's demon possession, of course, tells Mark's readers that Jesus's exorcism or healing of this man is extremely miraculous and compassionate. Thus the details of how severely possessed the Gerasene demoniac was serve primarily to alert readers to how impossible his healing would have been by normal means, and to how Jesus's power to perform miracles exceeded what most readers

---

3. Pervo, *Profit*, 12–85.

would have imagined. In order to heal this man, Jesus casts out not merely a single demon but (as the man's name suggests) thousands.

Secondarily, Mark's readers get a bit of entertainment from the demoniac's extraordinary behavior before his exorcism, which shows just how powerful the multiple demons were. And these demons, having inhabited a man in an unclean place, ask to enter unclean animals—pigs—rather than be in the presence of Jesus (5:11–13). The unclean nature of the region of the Gerasenes is illustrated once more by its inhabitants' asking Jesus to leave their area (5:17): now deprived of their unclean animals, the Gerasenes do not wish to become followers of Jesus in any way! Despite their evil power over the man whom they possessed, this power is far exceeded by Jesus's power. After the former demoniac has been restored to normality (5:15), this miracle story includes Jesus's and his disciples' boarding their boat in order to return to the land of Israel (5:17–18).

Through the lenses of form criticism, one can easily see the following:

The setting of the miracle, 5:1

The need for the miracle, 5:2–5

The dialogue between Jesus and the demons, 5:6–12

The performance of the miracle, 5:13

The crowd reaction, 5:14–17

The exit of Jesus and the apostles, 5:18–19

The final condition of the man who was healed, 5:20

Every miracle story in the Gospels does not feature all these elements; this is the miracle story that includes all of the traditional parts of a miracle story and a couple of extra elements.[4] Miracle stories in all the Gospels, and particularly in Mark, are fundamentally stories that raise the question of Jesus's divine identity, as illustrated by his unique ability to do the miraculous during his earthly life. This is both their literary and their theological functions.

---

4. In miracle stories from Matthew's Gospel, after the crowd reaction, the crowd itself often introduces a christological question: Jesus's miracle just then narrated causes onlookers to entertain queries such as "Who is this, that does [some deed of power]?" See most notably Matt 8:27.

Healings of Jairus's Daughter and the Woman with a Hemorrhage (5:21-43)

This passage is well known, not least for the fact that it includes one miracle story sandwiched inside another. The fact that this passage includes one miracle story intercalated (the technical term) between the parts of the other miracle story shows literary creativity on the part of the author/compiler/editor of Mark. The first miracle story, the one about the daughter of Jairus, begins with a dialogue between Jairus and Jesus, in which Jairus asks Jesus to come and lay his hands on his daughter, as she is dying. This dialogue between Jesus and Jairus gives the setting of the miracle: it establishes for the readers the fact that the little girl was mortally ill and that the crowd following Jesus took an interest in the little girl's healing (5:22-24).

As Jesus and the others are walking towards where the sick little girl is, a woman with a hemorrhage, who had heard of Jesus and had faith in his ability to heal her (5:25-27), moves close to Jesus to touch the cloak he was wearing, believing that if she could just touch his cloak (5:28) she would be saved from her disease. She does touch his cloak, and Jesus is aware of this (5:30), and immediately she is healed (5:29). Notably, Jesus's response to this woman is, "Daughter, your faith has saved you. Go in peace and be healed of your disease" (5:34).

The original miracle story then resumes in 5:35 with a dialogue in which Jairus is informed that his young daughter has died. Jesus hears this news, and instructs the synagogue leader: "Do not fear; only believe" (5:36). In both miracle stories there is an emphasis on faith. The fact that Jairus's daughter has already died emphasizes the impossibility of her healing by human means: now it can take place only by divine intervention. As far as Jesus is concerned, she is merely sleeping (5:39), which is an ancient euphemism for death. The Gospel of Mark shows Jesus giving the order in Aramaic for the girl to arise (5:41), and Jesus takes her by the hand and she rises, now alive. Jesus orders the parents not to say anything to anyone else about her being raised from death, and orders them to give the girl something to eat (5:43). This final detail signifies not only her recovery from sickness and death but also her return to normal life. In both miracle stories, the typical form is visible. This includes the setting of the miracle, both geographically and situationally, followed often by a dialogue between Jesus and others, which gives further details about the situation in which healing was needed; then Jesus performs the miracle, and the proof that it has been effective is provided for readers—after which, quite often, the onlookers or the crowds react to the miracle. The fact that the form of miracle stories seems to be cross-cultural may well point to the miracle story's going back to oral tradition. And so, as we read and interpret miracle stories in Mark, as well as other miracle stories in other biblical and extrabiblical gospels, we should be interested in how early such miracle stories or miraculous experiences were passed down in oral tradition, before they became part of the written Gospel of Mark that we now possess.

To make a long story short, we are not just interested in the stories in the text of Mark; we are also interested in the tradition—both oral and written—that predated the text. We are interested in this early tradition because we are interested in what the earliest church (or at least the early church) remembered and handed down about Jesus. This is a legitimate historical and theological concern. That miracle stories are so firmly established in the written Gospels that we now possess, starting with Mark, continuing with Matthew, Luke, and John (where only seven miracles are recounted), indicates that if the historical Jesus somehow did not perform miracles, the fact that the Gospels do indeed contain multiple miracle stories would require a rational explanation for how and why late first-century people made these stories up out of thin air. If they had done that, such fabrications would have opened up Christian belief to the charge by nonbelievers in Jesus that Jesus had been a magician. Such a critique of Jesus would not have been a charge that first-century Christ-followers would have chosen to evoke or to have to refute. Of course, we in the postmodern world do not know how Jesus did miracles. One thing of which we can be sure is that miracle stories were absolutely, positively part of the early tradition of Jesus's deeds. Both the oral tradition and the later, written tradition of the deeds of Jesus have come to us from the first century. Stories about healings could neither have circulated orally nor have been written down carrying our twenty-first-century perspectives about disease and recovery. So, the miracle stories of the first century CE are what they are. We should get real about the fact that the perspectives of those who compiled and edited them and our own perspectives are not the same.

The Rejection of Jesus in His Hometown (6:1–6a)

These few verses portray Jesus in the synagogue in Nazareth, the village where he grew up. Jesus, who had become known and sought after elsewhere in Galilee, now came to the congregation in which he had become an adult, in the context of his family—a context that included his brothers and sisters, and his previous participation in the family business of carpentry. Yet instead of his fellow Nazarenes' being proud of one of their sons, as they should have been, people in the village derided him and "took offense at him" (6:3).

Those of us who have read the literature of the modern world or the Middle Ages or the ancient world are fully aware that writings that describe what people do routinely include unfavorable as well as favorable portrayals. Stories, both oral and written, include narratives of "good guys" and "bad guys." One of the things that makes the Gospel According to Mark so memorable is that the twelve apostles, as well as other people, are repeatedly described in very unfavorable ways. This phenomenon will increase as we move from this part of the Gospel of Mark towards the passion narrative (and even to the story of the empty tomb in 16:1–8 and especially in 16:8).

Here in 6:1–6a we have unnamed villagers who dwelt in Nazareth along with Jesus's family, and who upon hearing Jesus teach in the synagogue, choose to join the chorus of naysayers. So, at least we can note that not only are Jesus's disciples cast in a generally unfavorable light: so also are the villagers in Nazareth. This appears to me to be a historical detail from the life of Jesus, likely remembered in the early church: Jesus came and preached in various towns and villages in Galilee, where he was quite well received, with the singular and jarring exception of his hometown. There would have been no reason whatsoever to make up the details of the rejection of Jesus by the people in Nazareth. Thus, this narrative seems just as historical as it was unfortunate and unjustified. What was the point of the Nazarenes' making dumb comments and asking loaded questions: "Where did this guy come by this? And what wisdom has been bestowed on this one, so that such deeds of power have happened at his hands? Is not this man a carpenter, the son of Mary and the brother of James and Joses and Judah and Simon? And aren't his sisters here with us?" (6:2–3 my trans.). This passage could be interpreted in more than one way. A more favorable way might be for the villagers to have wondered aloud just where and how Jesus got his learning, since they had grown up in the same village and in the same synagogue. A less favorable interpretation, however, is encouraged by the addition of the final words of 6:3: "And they took offense at him." So, a less favorable slant on the questions of 6:2–3a is encouraged by the "offense" of 6:3b. Villagers in Nazareth become part of the opposition to Jesus—and they are alone in this opinion among villagers in Galilee. The writer of Mark is pulling no punches here; nor does the writer pull punches elsewhere in this gospel, as we will see especially in the passion narrative. The final blow to Nazareth's reputation comes in 6:6a: "And he was amazed at their unbelief." Even given the unbelief of the people in the synagogue in Nazareth, Jesus did not fail to "lay hands on a few sick people" so that they were cured (6:5). None of the more spectacular miracles, such as the exorcism of one or more demons, as in 5:1–20, or the stilling of the storm as in 4:35–41, were done in Nazareth—precisely because of the villagers' refusal to believe in Jesus. Yet the readers of Mark are not left with a negative impression of Jesus and his power, but a negative impression of Nazareth, in contradistinction to other Galilean towns.

Authorizing the Twelve (6:6b–13)

Perhaps the writer of Mark means to tell the readers that Jesus's rejection at Nazareth is the reason that Jesus left his hometown and sent out his disciples to country places elsewhere in Galilee. This story describes the equipment that the Twelve are not to bring along with them: bread, bag, money, or a second tunic. Since they will be traveling on all kinds of surfaces, sandals will be needed. The author of Mark underlines for the readers that neither Jesus nor the Twelve did miracles by means of any magic or special equipment. It was the power of God alone, focused through the person of Jesus, the Son of God, that caused the miracles to take place.

Various Opinions About Jesus (6:14–16)

These three verses both introduce the flashback about the death of John the Baptizer which follows and also convey to readers various popular misunderstandings of Jesus. Two of the four understandings of Jesus associated him with John the Baptizer, and two of them associated Jesus with the prophet Elijah or "one of the prophets of old" (6:15). The most significant thing that can be said here is that these three verses record the diversity of opinions or thoughts about Jesus, which we will see repeated in 8:28–29, and the opinions of "people" stated there by Jesus's disciples include the same associations with John the Baptizer, Elijah, or "one of the prophets." It would not be difficult for us to speculate that there were popular opinions alive as late as 70 CE that continued to associate Jesus with John the Baptizer or Elijah or some other prophet about which Jesus-believers heard and read in the Septuagint or the Hebrew Bible. This passage causes the readers of Mark to understand that multiple opinions about Jesus have always existed, even during Jesus's natural lifetime, as well as after his death and resurrection. The best-known person who is portrayed as associating Jesus with a resurrected John the Baptizer is none other than Herod Antipas, the son of Herod the Great and Malthace.

The Murder of John the Baptizer (6:17–29)

This passage can be called a flashback because it gives a detailed historical narrative, detailing how and why the death of John the Baptizer took place. This flashback illustrates the statement of Herod, "John, whom I beheaded, has been raised" (6:16), as it also illustrates the earlier verse, "Some were saying, 'John the Baptizer has been raised from the dead'" (6:14). The writer of Mark wants to connect the sending or commissioning of the Twelve to the death of John the Baptizer. John was in the tradition of the prophets, and he baptized Jesus, who stood to some extent in the same prophetic tradition. Jesus appointed the Twelve, and they were his closest followers. They not only heard his teaching: they saw and participated in his miracles. So, the material in Mark about John the Baptizer emphasizes the continuity between John the Baptizer and Jesus, which was continued still further by the Twelve. And John the Baptizer himself had connections with the prophets, which is what Mark 1:2–6 is all about. John was none other than "the voice of one crying in the wilderness: 'Prepare the way of the Lord, make his paths straight,'" as the famous quotation in 1:3 of Isa 40:3 put it. It is very notable that "the Lord" to whom Isa 40:3 referred was God, meaning that God was coming back to be with Israel, indeed in Israel, as the Babylonian exile was ending. What John the Baptizer does in Mark 1:4–11 is also to "prepare the way of the Lord," and in this case "the Lord" means Jesus. The flashback here, later in the Gospel of Mark, to the death and to the last part of the life of John the Baptizer reminds Mark's readers of the faithful and distinctive ministry that John carried out, even denouncing Herod Antipas's marriage to Herodias, the wife of his brother Philip. And so, the murder of John the Baptizer at Herod's command is an illustration of the cost of the truth-telling that John did, and John's death foreshadows the death of Jesus. As we will see, there was no legal proceeding justifying the murder of John the Baptizer, while there was a trial of sorts at which Jesus was condemned to die—but only after Pontius Pilate had asked the crowd in Jerusalem what he, the Roman governor, should do with Jesus. So the unjust death of John the Baptizer foreshadowed the unjust death of Jesus of Nazareth. This underlines, for the readers of Mark, the supreme seriousness of both John the Baptizer and Jesus—with their explicit and strong roots in the ministries of the Hebrew prophets.

The Apostles Return (6:30–31)

These two verses, along with 6:32–34, provide the temporal and geographical setting to the famous miracle story where five thousand people were fed. Verse 31 in particular describes what the ministry of Jesus and the ministries of the Twelve were like: they were tired and they needed rest. Jesus was a supremely popular preacher in Galilee, and it was perhaps an exaggeration to say that Jesus and the apostles did not even have time to eat (6:31). We are not told in 6:30–31 that the apostles had carried food along with them to the wilderness place although their having brought provisions would not be a surprise. People who had common sense would know to travel with food: if they planned to move by land or sea away from cities or towns, they would need to bring food along. Thus, the tradition of the miracle story in 6:32–44 (as well as its parallels in the other three Gospels) was not that Jesus provided food for his apostles, but that he provided food for the large crowd of five thousand people. The wilderness place to which Jesus traveled with his apostles appears to have been a place in the country along the edge of the Sea of Galilee; the crowds who came were evidently from the towns around the sea (which was in fact a lake); thus, they likely lived not far away from the sea. Perhaps they got most of their food from fishing, so their proximity to the lake would have been a good thing. Thus it is not difficult to imagine that in these little towns the word of Jesus's presence, along with his reputation as a healer, would spread quickly.

The Feeding of the Five Thousand (6:32–44)

It is well known that the narrative of the Feeding of the Five Thousand is the single miracle story that appears in all four of the Gospels in the New Testament.[5] As they are usually divided up, miracle stories include

---

5. In addition to Mark 6:32–34, it appears in Matt 14:13–21, Luke 9:10b–17, and John 6:1–15.

healing miracles, nature miracles, and miracles of provision; this one is a miracle of provision. As a miracle story, its form-critical analysis is straightforward. The situational setting of the miracle is found in 6:32–34: Jesus, the disciples, and the crowd were out in the wilderness, and their time together had been extended because Jesus "began to teach them many things" (6:34). So perhaps it was partly due to Jesus's lengthy teaching out in what was normally a lonely place that there needed to be provided some food for the crowd. There is a dialogue in 6:35–38, giving further information about the impossibility of providing food to the crowd by normal means. Only five loaves of bread and two fish could not possibly feed even a small crowd, much less five thousand people (6:44)—the surprising detail that is saved until the end of this story. The performance of the miracle is in 6:39–41. It includes Jesus's order of the crowds to sit down or recline in groups on the green grass (6:39–40). Jesus took the loaves and gave them to disciples to distribute; he also divided up the two fish (6:41). The proof of the miracle is in 6:42–44, where the people all ate and were full, and there were collected twelve baskets of fragments of bread and fish, five thousand men having been fed with this small amount of modest food. Yet the five thousand were satisfied: they had eaten their fill and there was food left over. The large number of persons who were fed is part of what makes this story a miracle story.

In some places, there has been a rewriting of this story that many people who went to Sunday schools many years ago have been taught. This radical reworking of the story holds that Jesus did not do anything miraculous, as far as multiplication of the loaves or fish. It seems that Jesus preached "the fatherhood of God and the brotherhood of man" so that the hard hearts of his hearers were softened. The people had actually carried food with them into the wilderness, because they knew it might be a long time before they returned to their homes. They hid their food in their loose-fitting clothing (after all, didn't people in the Bible wear bathrobes?), and as they were now feeling generous, they were so moved by Jesus's teaching that they shared all their food. In this banal alteration of the miracle story, at its center is no longer a miracle of provision by Jesus but a transformation of the hearts of Jesus's hearers. This wishy-washy rewriting of the feeding of the five thousand, of course, features a liberal Jesus who does not actually do anything miraculous. This rendering of the story is not a legitimate or respectable interpretation, but a ridiculously misleading rewrite. It completely defeats the purpose of the formulation and preservation of the best-known miracle story in the New Testament, which was to teach the readers about Jesus's power and compassionate intention to perform miracles during his earthly life and ministry, precisely while he was teaching his disciples and others. In response to the popular rewrite of this miracle story, one should certainly ask this historical question: If Jesus did not perform miracles, why were the first-century writers, compilers, and editors of the Gospels so certain that he did?

Walking on the Water (6:45–52)

After the famous miracle of provision, the Gospel of Mark adds a nature miracle in 6:45–52. The placement of this miracle here raises a question for interpreters of Mark. The question is whether this miracle really did happen immediately after the feeding of the five thousand, which was in the wilderness near the Sea of Galilee, so that its geographical setting was not a detail simply made up by Mark.

This deed of power combines several themes that we can see elsewhere in Mark. First, Jesus wished to be alone so that he could pray (6:46). Jesus and his disciples, instead of being together as they usually were, are separated from each other. Worse for the disciples, as they attempt to cross the Sea of Galilee to arrive at the other side, the wind is against them so they have trouble rowing in the direction of the shore (6:47). The separation between Jesus and his disciples, however, is overcome by Jesus's walking towards the boat, actually on top of the surface of the water. Since it was the "fourth watch of the night," meaning the wee hours of the morning, the disciples thought the figure coming towards them on top of the water was a *phantasma*, some ghost or spirit, and they cried out in fear (6:49). Jesus calms their fears when he speaks words of comfort to them (6:50). This story is a nature miracle, and it is practically a double miracle: Jesus calms the fears of the disciples in the boat, and Jesus causes the wind to cease. The motif of the calming of the disciples' fears is, in a form-critical analysis of this miracle story, a proof to the reader that the miracle of the stilling of the sea really did take place. A result of the disciples' witnessing this nature miracle, even though Jesus also brings calm to the sea and calm to their emotions, is that the disciples are "utterly astonished" (6:51 my trans.). This is analogous to the crowd reaction in many miracle stories: the onlookers see that the miracle took place, and so they are amazed. This is another literary demonstration to the readers that the miracle being narrated really did happen. There were actual witnesses: it was not just a story made up. Yet the story ends with one more Markan touch, namely, the misunderstanding of the Twelve, even though they had seen the miracle with their own eyes. Their misunderstanding, Mark says, is due to the hardening of their hearts (6:52), a well-known motif from the Hebrew Bible. So, quite ironically, this unusual miracle story combines the disciples' initial obedience to Jesus's order to get in the boat (6:45) and go across the Sea of Galilee, and their failure to recognize Jesus as he walks on the water. This failure to recognize Jesus (6:49) may foreshadow the disciples' reluctance to believe in the resurrection even when it is told to them (16:5–8) in the final paragraph of the Gospel of Mark.

Gennesaret (6:53–56)

Eventually Jesus and the Twelve, as the result of their eventful sea crossing, do reach the northwest shore of the Sea of Galilee. The last four verses of Mark 6 describe healings that Jesus was called upon to do. By this point in Mark, Jesus is famous in Galilee for his ability to do healing miracles. Wherever Jesus goes, in either "villages or cities or farms" or "in the marketplaces" (6:56), healing is sought by people who come to where Jesus was, so that even if they would only "touch the edge of his cloak, they might be healed." These healings are more than a single healing miracle story; they summarize a number of healings, indicating Jesus's extreme popularity in out-of-the-way places near the Sea of Galilee. That people could be healed by touching the edge of Jesus's clothing indicates the extreme power to heal that Jesus had, of which Mark's readers have learned throughout this section, and not least in the exorcism of the Gerasene demoniac in 5:1–20. We note, of course, that Jesus uses the power to exorcise and to heal in order to bring health to people who were demonized or otherwise ill. There is no record of Jesus's use of his power to heal to enrich himself or his disciples, although we are not told how Jesus and his disciples obtained food to eat. What has been presented in Mark so far has emphasized Jesus's altruism: his offering his ministry of healing, preaching, and teaching as free gifts to those who asked for it and those who would listen to him.

6

Defilement and More Miracle Stories
Mark 7:1—8:26

THIS SECTION OF MARK takes the readers up to what can be thought of as the halfway mark in this gospel, namely, to chapter 8, verse 26. In Mark 8:27–30 we will read the confession of Peter, in which the apostle Peter is the first to confess that Jesus is the Messiah. Immediately after that, in 8:31–33, Jesus foretells his suffering and death, commonly called his passion. So after 8:26, the content of the Gospel of Mark will change so that the rest of Mark focuses almost completely on the suffering and death of Jesus.

What Defiles a Person (7:1–23)

This passage is a stunning indictment of "Pharisees and scribes" by Jesus, and, like much of what the Hebrew prophets preached, Jesus's words articulate a distinct position in a debate between him and other Jews, just as the book of Amos portrays the heated dialogue between the prophet Amos himself and Amaziah, the priest at the temple in Bethel in the northern kingdom of Israel.[1] Obviously neither Amos nor Amaziah was against Israelite religion, but Amos made justice the primary criterion for judging Israel's covenant loyalty to Yahweh, rather than ritual conformity. The

---

1. See especially Amos 7:10–17. Amos 2:6–11 records prophecies against Israel, paralleling the prophecies against other nations of the ancient Near East, including Judah at 2:4–5.

insistence on the priority of justice as a virtue and a goal within Judaism was common among the prophets. Jesus came by this perspective quite honestly: it is likely that he was taught it by the rabbi at the synagogue in Nazareth. The same may well have been true for John the Baptizer. Prioritizing justice did not by any means represent an attack on Judaism, but rather served as a call from certain Jews to other Jews to understand and to practice Judaism according to its sacred traditions of observing the Torah of Moses and keeping faith with the prophets—whose major issue was justice.

This prophetic criticism of the rituals of religion stands behind Mark 7:1–23. Like some of the prophets, Jesus both stood within the traditions of Judaism and was also critical of some of them. The prophets were not generally oriented towards ritual purity; they were strongly oriented towards moral purity.

In several of the Greek manuscripts of Mark 7:3–4, these two verses are set off from the verses surrounding them (7:2 and 5) by dashes. These dashes in Greek manuscripts at the beginning of 7:3 and at the end of 7:4 are represented by parentheses in English translations. It is as if the copyists and editors were saying to the early readers of Mark that 7:3–4 are not what Jesus actually said about "Pharisees and some of the scribes" (7:1), but are the author of Mark's rather dismissive comments on Jewish rules about handwashing and about washing bronze vessels. These two verses indicate to the readers of Mark that the Jerusalem tradition of Judaism, as then practiced, was in great contrast to the Judaism practiced by Jesus of Nazareth and his followers. Given that Jesus and his followers were from Galilee, the opposition of various Jerusalem Jews to them is not surprising.[2]

Some commentators divide this passage into two parts: 7:1–15 and 7:17–23. Verse 16, however, is missing from early manuscripts.[3] The fact

---

2. See especially Géza Vermes, *Jesus in His Jewish Context*, as well as Vermes, *Jesus and the World of Judaism*.

3. These manuscripts include such as Codex Sinaiticus, Codex Vaticanus, and several others, though it was present in Codex Alexandrinus, Codex Bezae Cantabrigiensis, Codex Koredethi, in the Byzantine manuscript tradition, and in the Syriac, Old Latin, and Vulgate versions. Thus, Constantin von Tischendorf's venerable *Novum Testamentum Graece, editio octava critica maior* (1869), the Nestle-Aland 28th edition (2012), and the United Bible Societies 5th edition (2014) omit it, while the massive, new *Novum Testamentum Graecum: editio critica maior* (2021) includes it in double square brackets, about which the Nestle-Aland 28th revised edition says, "The text enclosed in double square brackets cannot be considered authentic" (880). Verse 16 seems quite superfluous: "the one who has ears to hear, let that one hear!" This exhortation to listen is found elsewhere in the Gospels, but it seems out of place here.

that several early witnesses to the text of Mark omit it encourages us to think that this verse did not come from the author of Mark.

The passage 7:17–23 is different from the verses that precede it, in that in 7:1–16 Jesus is speaking with the general public, in the presence of "the Pharisees and some of the scribes who came from Jerusalem," yet in 7:17–23 Jesus is answering questions put to him privately by his disciples about "the parable" and is thus "in the house away from the crowd" (7:17). "The parable" referred to in 7:17 seems to be the saying in 7:14–15. This saying, that it is not the things which come from outside a person but the things that come from the inside of a person that defile that person, is not a piece of scriptural interpretation as 7:9–13 is. It is a type of wisdom saying. Instead of designating particular foods as having the property of defiling a person (7:19), Jesus claims that what truly makes a person unclean are the things that come "from within, from the human heart" (7:21), meaning evil thoughts, plans, and behaviors. The things that come from the outside, including foods, come into the body but go out again. Thus, since the foods that came into the body through eating then go out "into the sewer" (7:19), they no longer defile the person who eats them. Mark tells the readers that Jesus "declared all foods clean" (7:19). For the Jesus of the Gospel of Mark, the dietary laws of Judaism are of no consequence. The purity of which Jesus speaks is not about food or drink or even many other aspects of the physical world. Jesus advises his followers against the evil that comes from the human heart and results in evil behaviors, as enumerated in the catalogue of vices in 7:21–22. Thus, like the Hebrew prophets of old, Jesus identifies moral evil as the real evil.[4]

The Encounter with the Syrophoenician Woman (7:24–30)

This surprising passage has Matt 15:21–28 as its parallel, and the woman in the Matthew passage is a Canaanite, while she is a Syrophoenician in Mark.

---

4. On the relationship of the divine requirement of justice to the rest of the prophetic critique of Israel, see Eichrodt, *Theology of the Old Testament*, 1:356–81. On 1:356 Eichrodt commented, "*The prophetic preaching created a split within the nation* which separated membership of the true people of God from the mere fact of belonging to Israel, replacing this qualification with one based on the personal assumptions of the individual" (italics original). In other words, simply belonging to the people of Israel was not enough: one had to do what the God of Israel, the God of justice, commanded. It should not be difficult for us to see how close this perspective comes to the perspectives of both John the Baptizer and Jesus.

The Gospel of Luke does not contain this story. I believe it is fundamentally a miracle story, but it is a miracle story in which the most important element is the dialogue between the Syrophoenician woman and Jesus about whether he was going to heal her daughter or not. This very issue seems surprising to us, perhaps because we have heard the words of the familiar children's song "Jesus loves the little children, all the children of the world." St. Paul, of course, famously wrote, "In Christ there is neither Jew nor Greek, neither slave nor free person, neither male nor female" (Gal 3:28 my trans.), in the context of the circumcision controversy created by his enemies' infiltration of Galatian churches in his absence. Jesus's initial answer to the request for him to heal the Syrophoenician woman's daughter seems like the kind of answer that Christian writers in the late first and early second century would not want to associate with Jesus, let alone attribute to him—precisely because this response by Jesus equates being Syrophoenician with being a dog (7:27). Very surprisingly, this woman replies that "even dogs get what falls from the table when the children are eating" (7:28 my trans.). The Syrophoenician woman takes an ethnic insult from Jesus—comparing Syrophoenicians to dogs—and turns this insult on its ear. In effect, the woman says to Jesus, "Since we in the region of Tyre are not, as in your religion, the favored People of God, but are dogs, then treat us like household pets eating crumbs that fall from the children's table." It is true that the word *kynaria*, the diminutive form of *kyōn* ("dog"), appears here, so that it is possible to translate it as "little dogs" or "puppies" instead of "dogs" in 7:27–28. Fundamentally, however, even that translation cannot hide the fact that Jesus initially refuses to heal the woman's daughter precisely because she is not a fellow Jew, despite the fact that the Syrophoenician woman had heard about Jesus, and despite her daughter's having "an unclean spirit" (7:25). In this passage, it is the woman's quick comeback to Jesus's refusal to heal her daughter that causes Jesus to change his mind and effect the healing. Is it possible that the woman who encountered Jesus as she did, to try to get him to heal her daughter (who was not with her at the time), had almost as much an effect on Jesus as his healing did on the little girl? Jesus sent the woman away: "because of [your] word, go; the demon as come out of your daughter" (7:29 my trans.). The Gospel of Matthew places these additional words in Jesus's mouth, just before his proclamation of the little girl's healing: "O woman, great is your faith!" (15:28 my trans.), faith being a favorite theme of that gospel.

Yet the Gospel of Mark does not elaborate further on the fact that, at the request of a pagan woman in a pagan land, Jesus healed a little girl, except to point out that it was a healing that took place without the little girl's being present. This illustrates the power of Jesus to effect the exorcism, without using Aramaic words or gestures associated with healing. Jesus had previously encountered the man with innumerable demons—also in a pagan country—in Mark 5:1–20. But the exorcism in Mark 5 did not raise any issue about the fact that Jesus did an exorcism for a person who was not a fellow Jew. So both in Mark 5:1–20 and here in 7:24–30, the author or compiler of Mark wants to lay most of the emphasis on the power of Jesus to cast out demons, apparently thousands of them in Mark 5 and at long distance here in Mark 7. If the Gospel of Mark was written around 70 CE, this means that Gentile churches founded by Barnabas and Paul were already in existence. There were already plenty of Gentile Jesus-believers. They would have been very interested in Jesus's going outside Israel and then healing the Syrophoenician woman's daughter. In the exorcism of the Gerasene demoniac, the fact that the demoniac was besieged by as many as thousands of demons suggests that he was very much under the power of evil (or the Evil One). The demons are the ones who speak to Jesus. In contrast, this story in 7:24–30 says that the little girl has "an unclean spirit" but does not suggest that the girl in the region of Tyre was completely under the power of evil. In this story, the girl for whom healing is desired is not evil at all, but has been attacked by a demon which caused an illness. This miracle story, like others, portrays Jesus as fully in control of any of the powers of evil.

Other Healings (7:31–37)

In 7:31 Jesus exits the region of Tyre, goes through Sidon, and goes to the Sea of Galilee, into the midst of the regions of the Decapolis. He leaves one Gentile region to go into another one, the region of the "Ten Cities." He is confronted by a person in this region who was both deaf and mute. Other people ask Jesus to "lay his hand on him" for healing (7:31). Jesus here does not object to the healing of this Gentile man as he had to the exorcism of the Syrophoenician woman's daughter. In this miracle story, Jesus makes several gestures associated with healing: he lays his hand on the man, and after taking him to a different place in private, Jesus puts his fingers into the man's ears, and after spitting, touches his tongue, and looking to heaven he said "Ephphatha," which was Aramaic for "Be opened" (7:32–34). As the evident result of these gestures, the man's ears were opened, his tongue was loosened, and he spoke plainly (7:35). Jesus orders the onlookers to remain silent about the man's healing, but they did not obey this order. The crowd was "exceedingly amazed" so that they said, "He has done all things well: he indeed makes the deaf hear and the mute to speak" (7:37).

Wolfgang Roth, in his provocative book *Hebrew Gospel*, argued that the Gospel of Mark is modeled on the Elijah/Elisha cycle of miracle stories found in the Hebrew Bible (Old Testament) from 1 Kgs 17 through 2 Kgs 13. Very notably the greatest miracle worker in the Hebrew Bible was the prophet Elisha, who did sixteen miracles, while his predecessor and mentor, Elijah, did eight miracles. In the Gospel of Mark Jesus does sixteen miracles, and then after the sixteenth miracle—the same number of deeds of power that Elisha had done—the crowd proclaims about Jesus, "He has done all things well" (7:37). Then, there are eight more deeds of power in Mark, ending with Jesus's resurrection in 16:1–8.[5] Roth notes the importance of the numerical relationships: Elijah did eight deeds of power, and then Elisha did sixteen deeds of power. Very significantly, Elisha had also asked that he would inherit a "double share" of Elijah's spirit in 2 Kgs 2:9. Evidently the bestowal of the double share of Elijah's spirit did happen. I certainly do not think that the number of Jesus's deeds of power, which equals the total of Elijah's and Elisha's deeds of power combined, is an accident or a coincidence. Roth's book argues that this point of contact between the Gospel of Mark and the Elijah/Elisha cycle of stories in 1 and 2 Kings is one among several. Also very notable is the fact that in Mark's Gospel John the Baptizer is identified with Elijah, which suggests that for Mark Jesus corresponds to Elisha.

The Feeding of the Four Thousand (8:1–10)

The pattern identified by Wolfgang Roth and the Gospel of Mark's inclusion of eight more deeds of power after 7:37 also provides an excellent

---

5. Roth, *Hebrew Gospel*, 4–20. Roth comments: "As Elisha extends by eight Elijah's eight miracles, so now Jesus extends by another eight Elisha's sixteen. It is interesting that Jesus does not double the number of Elisha's miracles; direct continuity with the scriptural model is sought, and in this manner Jesus's mission is conceptualized and legitimated" (16–17). I suggest that another way of looking at the 16-plus-8 miracles is that Jesus's deeds of power are the equal or perhaps the reenactment of Elisha's and Elijah's deeds of power put together.

explanation for the feeding of the four thousand, which happens in Mark soon after the feeding of the five thousand in 6:32–44. The feeding of the four thousand, about a chapter and a half after the feeding of the five thousand, is the first deed of power after the crowd's recognition that Jesus "has done all things well" in 7:37. This deed along with the resurrection of Jesus in 16:1–8 and the six deeds of power between them, will bring the total of Jesus's deeds of power in Mark to twenty-four. It certainly seems clear that there was a robust supply of miracle stories in oral tradition (if not also in written form) available to Mark, so that the story of another miracle which consisted of feeding a crowd would not have been hard to come by.

Seeking a Sign (8:11–13)

This short passage illustrates the relations between Jesus and the Pharisees. Jesus has not yet entered Jerusalem, as he will do in 11:1–10, and yet the Pharisees are trying to debate with him, even in an otherwise unknown town called Dalmanutha (8:10). Jesus does not accede to their demand for a "sign from heaven," discerning that they are "testing him" (8:11). Jesus then criticizes them for their demanding a sign (8:12) and departs to the other side of the lake (8:13).

The Yeast of the Pharisees (8:14–21)

This passage opens with the Twelve having neglected to bring any food, except for a single loaf of bread, with them when they boarded the boat with Jesus. The readers of Mark are not told that the Twelve reported this lack of food to Jesus, yet Jesus initiates a conversation about bread when he warns them to beware "the yeast of the Pharisees and the yeast of Herod" (8:15). The disciples, however, think that Jesus is simply talking about their lack of bread (8:16), which means that they do not comprehend the larger meaning of Jesus's mentioning Pharisees and Herod. So Jesus says more: He asks if their hearts are hardened, or if they are completely oblivious to what is going on around them. He queries how much bread was left over from the feeding of the five thousand and the feeding of the four thousand, namely, twelve and seven baskets of bread respectively from those two deeds of power, which the disciples had witnessed. Jesus's point is that since he had done these two deeds of power, creating the equivalent of thousands of loaves of bread, there is little reason to discuss the relatively minor shortage of bread in the boat. Thus, the disciples are portrayed here as having little or no understanding of Jesus's larger purpose in doing deeds of power or in preaching the kingdom of God.

The Healing of a Blind Man (8:22–26)

This miracle story focuses the attention of readers on Jesus's techniques of healing the blind man. Rather than an emphasis on Jesus's identity as Son of God or on healing via exorcism of evil spirits, this story is unusual in that it emphasizes that Jesus took the blind man by the hand and led him out of the village of Bethsaida. At the end of the miracle story, Jesus orders the man, "Do not go into the village" (8:26). Jesus healed the man by putting his saliva on the man's eyes, yet the man's vision was not completely restored (8:24). Then, learning that the man could still not see well, Jesus "laid his hands on his eyes again, and [the man who was healed] saw clearly," and the second healing gesture caused his vision to come back completely (8:25).

Vincent Taylor in his landmark commentary on Mark points out important parallels between the structure of this miracle story and the healing of the deaf-mute in Mark 7:32–37: "In each case spittle is used and the laying on of hands; restoration is accomplished with some difficulty or in stages; and finally, in each instance a charge to maintain secrecy is imposed."[6] These parallels led some scholars to argue that the same event was narrated twice. Yet, as Taylor sees them, the details of both stories are so unusual, including the fact that the healings are done by Jesus with difficulty or in stages, that they have "a mark of historical truth,"[7] in that the early church would have been unlikely to make up the details of the difficulty Jesus had in doing the miracles. There are no parallels to these stories in Matthew and Luke. Thus, Taylor interprets the distinctiveness of these stories to weigh in favor of these two healings as actual historical events.

The First Half of Mark: Some Concluding Thoughts

In the Nestle-Aland *Novum Testamentum Graece*, 28th edition, there are seventy-three pages from Mark 1:1 to 16:8; there are other endings of Mark as well. These additional endings include the shorter ending of Mark

---

6. Taylor, *Gospel According to St. Mark*, 368.
7. Taylor, *Gospel According to St. Mark*, 369.

Defilement and More Miracle Stories

(which has neither chapter nor verse number) and 16:9–20; these additions constitute two more pages. From 1:1 to 8:26 there are thirty-five pages, and from 8:27 to 16:8 there are thirty-eight pages, so at 8:26 we are approximately halfway through the Gospel of Mark. This is a good opportunity to take stock of what we have experienced and learned so far.

The Gospel of Mark opens without a special birth story or any information about the parentage of Jesus or any details about how Jesus grew up in Galilee. We readers of Mark are not told how Jesus somehow became the divine Son of God, but his status as Son of God is clear from the story of his baptism and the voice from heaven in 1:11 proclaiming, "You are my beloved Son; in you I am well pleased." Note that Jesus is addressed by the voice from heaven (evidently God the Father) in the second person singular, so the readers of Mark are not told that anyone else heard that voice. We readers are told about Jesus's status as Son of God in the pages of Mark, yet the disciples whom Jesus calls at the lakeshore and elsewhere do not discern Jesus's divine status until the confession of Peter in 8:29—even though the demons already know what and who Jesus is. The second half of Mark, from 8:27 on, reveals more and more to the readers, who have already learned Jesus's true identity from the heavenly voice at Jesus's baptism. Of course from Mark 1:3, the quotation from Isa 40:3, in concert with the quotation in Mark 1:2, which is Mal 3:1, we learn that God is sending a messenger, and that this messenger, who will go "before your face" (1:2) is none other than a person who will "prepare the way of the Lord," who will "make his paths straight" (1:3). This messenger who goes before the Lord is none other than John the Baptizer, and in this case "the Lord" is in fact Jesus. So a major part of what happens in the Gospel of Mark is the gradual unfolding to the readers of what is important to know about Jesus. Jesus is not only God's beloved Son: he is also "the Lord."

Jesus, the beloved Son of God, came to proclaim that "the time is fulfilled, and the kingdom of God has come near" (1:15) to those who encounter Jesus's preaching and teaching. John the Baptizer became a martyr under King Herod, and his removal from the story in Mark makes room for Jesus to create a wider scope for his own ministry. According to Mark 1:2, John is the one who was "my [i.e., God's] messenger before your [i.e., Jesus's] face." His work was to "prepare the way of the Lord," namely Jesus (1:3). Before the murder of John the Baptizer by Herod Antipas, the Holy Spirit throws Jesus out into the wilderness to endure physical hardships including hunger and temptations by Satan for the familiar biblical number of forty days, and yet the divine presence is still mediated to Jesus in the wilderness through the ministry of angels (1:12–13). After these hardships and temptations in the wilderness (1:12) where John the Baptizer spent his time (1:3), Jesus is made ready for his ministry in Galilee which is so well summarized in 1:14–15: Jesus is "preaching the gospel of God and saying that the time is fulfilled and the kingdom of God has come near" (my trans.). Those who hear Jesus (and by extension, those who read or hear the Gospel of Mark) are to "repent and believe in the gospel." Yet, even after the divine voice in 1:11 and the brief summary in 1:15, the unfolding of Jesus in Mark has barely begun. The readers simply have not yet been told what this gospel, this "good news," actually is.

The unfolding of Jesus in Mark continues with the rather jarringly brief calling of the first four apostles by the lakeshore. The usual interpretation is that Jesus was omniscient, and so he knew exactly whom he should call and why. As I read Mark, it is not clear to me that Jesus is portrayed as omniscient in Mark. Thus, we readers of Mark should have an open mind as we try to make sense of what Mark says about those whom Jesus called as his twelve apostles. The proof of the rightness of Jesus's calling them to the ministry of apostleship must be discerned by carefully reading the entire text of Mark, from start to finish, rather than by looking only at part of chapter 1.

7

Predictions of Suffering, Death, and Resurrection

Mark 8:27—10:52

THIS SECTION OF MARK contains Jesus's three predictions of his suffering, death, and resurrection. These three predictions of the passion in Mark 8:31–34, 9:30–37, and 10:32–34 are paralleled in Matt 16:13–33, 17:22–23, and 20:17–28 as well as Luke 9:18–22, 9:43–48, and 18:31–34. The first of the three predictions by Jesus is prefaced by the confession of Peter. The confession of Peter is the event at which Peter, the first of the apostles to do so, says that Jesus is the Messiah.

The Confession of Peter (8:27–30)

This section appears to begin the second half of the Gospel of Mark. Mark seems to proceed, after the baptism of Jesus in 1:9–11, with its portrayal of the disciples as being in the dark about who and what Jesus is. Several disciples answer Jesus's question, "Who do people say that I am?" (8:27). Two of the answers given center on John the Baptizer and Elijah. This is one more indication from Mark of the importance of Jesus's relationship with John the Baptizer and with the Elijah/Elisha cycle of stories. Yet when Jesus asks his disciples the more important question, "Who do you say that I am?" only Peter gives an answer. Peter, alone among the disciples, knows that Jesus is the Messiah. Admittedly, the disciples and Jesus, according to Mark, have not made their entry into Jerusalem, and Jesus has not been acclaimed as Messiah there; this does not happen until 11:1–10. By that time, in Mark's presentation, the increased number of Jesus's followers seem certain that Jesus is the Messiah of Israel, meaning an anointed king in the line of David. By then, Jesus's identity as Messiah is public, while in 8:30 Jesus orders his disciples to tell no one who he is. Perhaps Jesus orders secrecy because he does not wish to be mobbed whenever he and his disciples go out and do ministry. Certainly, the secrecy motif emphasizes that, while the demons know who and what Jesus is from the moment they encounter him, most of Jesus's disciples—with the single exception of Peter—do not know who Jesus is, even as late as 8:27–28. Most of Jesus's disciples, as they are portrayed in Mark, learn about Jesus's messianic identity only by hearing it from the lips of Peter, not because they had discerned it for themselves.

This passage raises the issue of what was meant by "messiah," which is the better translation of *christos*, which has traditionally been translated "the Christ." Literally *mashiach* is Hebrew for "anointed one," and *christos* is Greek for the same word. Much has been written about who or what the messiah was, both before the discovery of the Dead Sea Scrolls in 1947 and since that time.[1] In general terms, one should understand that in the ancient Near East, kings were anointed rather than crowned. Hence, an "anointed one" would have been understood to be a person who was anointed as a king, a person who was not only anointed by a chief priest or other religious leader but adopted into a special sonship with God. Thus a messiah was understood to have a special relationship with God that others did not have. It would not be surprising for a person who was *Mashiach* (anointed) to be called "Son of God."

The First Prediction of the Passion (8:31–33)

This first prophecy of the suffering, death, and resurrection of Jesus takes place immediately after Peter has identified Jesus as the Messiah. In this prophecy, Jesus informs his disciples about what kind of Messiah he is and will be. Jesus understands his ministry as the Messiah as a ministry that includes intense suffering and his sacrifice of his life. This messiahship will then be capped off by Jesus's being resurrected on the third day after his death. This information about what is in store for Jesus's future is evidently

---

1. See especially the classic book by Sigmund Mowinckel, *He That Cometh*.

Predictions of Suffering, Death, and Resurrection

horrifying to the disciples. Peter refuses to accept this prophecy of Jesus's doom from Jesus himself. As a result of Peter's refusal to take Jesus at his word, even after Peter had correctly identified Jesus as the Messiah, Jesus speaks quite harshly to Peter, saying, "Get behind me, Satan!" (8:33).

It is interesting that "the elders and the chief priests and the scribes" are listed in 8:31 as the ones who will put Jesus on trial, a trial which will result in Jesus's being put to death. The notion that the Jewish leaders in Jerusalem at the time of Jesus were responsible for his death has, quite unfortunately, persisted in the Christian tradition. The movement that put Jesus on trial may well have started with those Jewish leaders in Jerusalem at that time, yet the actual trial that did result in the sentence of death was a trial by the Roman prefect Pontius Pilate.[2] Jesus's executioners were Roman soldiers, and they carried out the order of the Roman prefect. Joachim Gnilka points out in his excellent book *Jesus of Nazareth: Message and History* that the Gospels were written in such a way that they tend to exonerate the Roman occupation government for the death of Jesus, shifting the blame for Jesus's death away from the Romans to Jews who were within the hierarchy in Jerusalem.[3]

The three predictions of the suffering, death, and resurrection of Jesus in Mark 8, 9, and 10, emphasize to the readers the seriousness of Jesus as he pursues his mission. They also tell readers that Jesus knew that he was going to "give his life as a ransom for many" (10:45) and that his journey to Jerusalem, as dangerous as it was for him, was a course of action that Jesus actually chose. Thus, those who would become followers of Jesus, wherever they are and whenever they live, are exhorted to be ready to suffer the martyrdom that Jesus experienced. This is what it meant to "take up your cross and follow me" (8:34).

When St. Paul wrote one of his earlier letters to Corinthian Jesus-believers, he made a detailed refutation of those who denied the resurrection of Jesus (1 Cor 15:12-19). At the beginning of what Paul argued in that Corinthian letter was Paul's statement from tradition that he had previously taught the Corinthians: "that Christ died for our sins in accordance with the scriptures, and that he was buried and that he was raised on the third day in accordance with the scriptures" (1 Cor 15:3-4). Thus, by the time Paul was writing to Corinthian Jesus-believers in the 50s CE, the death, burial, and resurrection of Jesus have already become matters of taught tradition,

---

2. Gnilka, *Jesus of Nazareth*, 290-318.
3. Gnilka, *Jesus of Nazareth*, 301.

and these traditions embedded in this part of 1 Corinthians appear to have existed about twenty years before the Gospel According to Mark was written. So by the time the Gospel of Mark was written, the tradition of belief in Jesus's death, burial, and resurrection is a given. It certainly appears to be a foundational tradition upon which other Christian traditions were based.

Taking Up One's Cross (8:34—9:1)

One of the most famous sayings of Jesus is for his followers to "take up his cross and follow me." (The saying in the text of Mark 8:34 is in the third person masculine singular: "his.") This is a difficult, indeed horrifying, saying of Jesus. The original context of the saying appears to be an exhortation by Jesus to follow Jesus in his martyrdom. The parallels to this verse in the other Synoptic Gospels are Matt 16:24 and Luke 9:23. Very notably, the Lukan parallel adds "according to the day" or "daily" to the saying of "taking up one's cross." This means that for Luke Jesus was not talking about death by Roman execution here, as in Mark and Matthew, but about the daily living of life as his followers. This was a significant shift away from the death of martyrdom to continuing to live one's life as a serious follower of Jesus. This shift away from the normative prospect of martyrdom for Christians in the first century is a phenomenon of the Gospel of Luke. Mark is clear that believers in Jesus need to be willing and able to give their lives as part of the brutal reality of Roman occupation of Israel; believers in Jesus need to not be "ashamed of [Jesus] and of [his] words in this adulterous and sinful generation" (8:38).

Mark is even clearer about the prospect of the second coming of Christ happening within the lifetimes of some of those hearers of Jesus: "Truly I tell you, there are some standing here who will not taste death until they see that the kingdom of God has come with power" (9:1). Hence the author or compiler of the Gospel of Mark expected the second coming of Jesus to be quite soon. This expectation in the Gospel of Mark contrasts sharply with the expectation in the Gospel of Luke. Although the writer of Luke used Mark as a written source, this use of Mark did not mean that Luke shared the same perspective on the second coming of Christ or on other important theological matters. Just as the Gospel of Mark has a theology, so also do the Gospels of Matthew, Luke, and John.

Predictions of Suffering, Death, and Resurrection

The Transfiguration of Jesus (9:2–13)

This enigmatic passage has puzzled many generations of readers of Mark. It is hard to be certain what was being narrated or what the narration of the transfiguration means in the Gospel of Mark. The transfiguration seems to have something to do with Christology (with defining who Jesus the Messiah is and what he is to do). God, who speaks from the cloud, now proclaims, within the hearing of Peter, James, and John, that Jesus is "my Son, the Beloved," and he adds, "Listen to him!" (9:7). This is an affirmation of Jesus as Son of God to the inner circle of Jesus's disciples. It is in some contrast to God's affirmation of Jesus at his baptism as "my Son, the beloved," which, in Mark 1:11, only Jesus heard. Jesus's divine sonship only Jesus and the demons knew, and then at the confession of Peter in 8:27 also Peter knows, with a lot of silence from the other disciples. Now at the transfiguration in Mark, the entire inner circle of disciples is given insider knowledge of Jesus as Son of God. By extension the readers of Mark are given this insider knowledge as well. Since they first read it at 1:11, there have been many miraculous deeds of power that could only have been done supernaturally. The readers of Mark have not been told by chapter 9 whether the other nine disciples of Jesus have also come to believe that Jesus is Son of God.

The transfiguration narrative in Mark does not mention the suffering and death of Jesus, while the parallel narrative in Luke 9:31 tells its readers that Moses and Elijah were speaking with Jesus "about his exodus, which he was about to fulfill in Jerusalem" (my trans.). The overall impression of the transfiguration story is that the three disciples were being allowed to see Jesus as he truly was, with the heavenly glory of his divine sonship now briefly visible to the inner circle of disciples. Perhaps this was meant to confirm them in their faith (or solely Peter's faith) that Jesus was in fact the Messiah, and by extension this narrative confirms the readers' faith in Jesus as well. Mark 9:9 shows that the secrecy motif, so well attested in Mark, is found yet one more time when even the inner circle of the disciples have heard the voice of God from the cloud, both identifying Jesus as Son of God and exhorting those present, "Listen to him!" Jesus orders these three disciples to keep the secret of his divine sonship until after he has risen from the dead, so this is one more prophecy of the resurrection. In v. 10, these disciples still don't understand Jesus, in that they still do not understand what Jesus meant by "rising from the dead." Yet ironically given this misunderstanding in Mark, it is the apostles of Jesus, according to Acts of the Apostles 1:21–22, who will become the primary witnesses of Jesus's resurrection from death. But the affirmation of the apostles as witnesses to the resurrection is very prominently absent from the Gospel of Mark, since Mark 1:1—16:8 has no resurrection appearances. Also, the women who come to anoint the dead body of Jesus at the tomb and meet the angels who inform them of Jesus's resurrection do not say anything to the apostles about Jesus's having risen from death (16:8). The readers of Mark might well expect the women at the empty tomb to speak with great confidence about Jesus's resurrection, but they do not. The apostles in the Gospel of Mark are not even told by either an angel or the women who visited Jesus's tomb that Jesus rose from death.

Back in 9:11–13, the writer of Mark shifts the attention of the readers away from the death of Jesus for a moment to the important matter of who Jesus was, especially in relationship to John the Baptizer, by comparing John and Jesus to Elijah and Elisha. Elijah was the necessary forerunner to Elisha, who ended up doing twice as many deeds of power as Elijah. The coming of Elijah and later of Elisha was part of God's plan for the renewal of Israel. The deeds of power that these two prophets did were nothing less than signs of God's supporting these great prophets. The deeds of power done by Elijah and Elisha were not only willed by God but also fully empowered by God. This was the message of the transfiguration in 9:2–10. The naming of Elijah, the forerunner of the greater prophet Elisha, reminds the original readers of Mark of the connection between Elijah and Elisha, which was, in Mark's perspective, actualized in the first century CE as the connection between John the Baptizer and Jesus. Though Elijah was to come first, as Mark says, "to restore all things," it was nonetheless true that sufferings were to happen to both John the Baptizer and Jesus.

In 9:12 Jesus is identified as "the Son of Man," a somewhat mysterious title about which much has been written. Enigmatically, just as John the Baptizer suffered and was put to an unjust death (6:14–29), so the same fate would also happen to Jesus (14:1—15:47). Yet in Jesus's case, death was not to be the end: Jesus rose from death (16:1–8), the final outcome which neither the women at the empty tomb nor the apostles would truly comprehend on the day of Jesus's resurrection.

Ironically, the fact that "the scribes say that Elijah must come first" (9:11), the subject of the apostles' question to Jesus, demonstrates that the scribes, as well versed in Scripture as they are, have gotten some of the details about the coming of Jesus quite right. The scribes, of course, would have denied that John the Baptizer was to be identified with Elijah. Their statement that Elijah must come first, part of Jewish tradition about the Messiah, was likely meant to prove that Jesus was in no sense the Messiah. From Mark's perspective, however, the scribes' not linking John the Baptizer with Elijah constitutes a major failure. What may well have been meant to show from the scribal viewpoint that Jesus was not the Messiah, turns out—in the perspective of the Gospel of Mark—to show that actually Jesus is indeed the Anointed One who came to Israel precisely because God the Father sent him to renew the people of God. The scribes, therefore were right about the fact that Elijah did precede the coming of the Anointed One, while they were not to perceive that John the Baptizer, in their own time, did fulfill the role of Elijah and so became the forerunner of the Messiah.

Jesus Exorcizes a Boy (9:14–29)

From the perspective of modern medicine, the boy who is the subject of this healing miracle in this passage was afflicted with epilepsy. He had had, and continued to have, seizures. Modern medicine would explain his condition by way of an electrical or other abnormality in the boy's brain. Mark 9:14–29, however, was written from an ancient point of view, not a modern one. The typical parts of miracle stories are present in this passage: the setting of the miracle, the dialogue (in this story, quite an extended dialogue), the performance of the miracle, and the reaction of the onlookers. The setting of this miracle in 9:14–15 is almost immediately after the transfiguration in 9:2–8; Jesus and the three disciples are coming down the mountain. In the dialogue of 9:19–24, the readers learn the extent of the boy's illness: he is unable to speak and (as also revealed in the performance of the miracle in 9:25) cannot hear. The "spirit" the boy had causes him to convulse as it comes out (9:26), and the boy seems dead. Jesus takes the boy by the hand in 9:27 and raises him up. A final dialogue between the disciples and Jesus introduces the pronouncement, "This kind [of spirit] can come out only through prayer," to which many manuscripts add "and fasting" (9:29).

This miracle story as a whole informs the readers of the compassionate nature of Jesus. Even given the heavenly presence in the transfiguration in 9:2–8, Jesus had not become so otherworldly that he could not or would not heal a young person in a pathetic state caused by deafness, the inability to speak, and seizures. These conditions cause the boy's father to bring him to Jesus. Jesus responds to the faith of the father, a faith which is perhaps limited and partial: he asks Jesus to heal his son in these words, "if you are able to do anything, have pity on us and help us" (9:22). Jesus then says, "All things can be done for the one who believes" (9:23), to which the father responds, evidently not with complete faith, "I believe—help my unbelief!" (9:24). Fundamentally this passage portrays not only the power of Jesus but also his compassion for a family and a child with serious needs.

The Second Prediction of the Passion (9:30–32)

In this brief second prediction of the passion and resurrection, Jesus declares that he will be "betrayed into human hands," resulting in his being killed, and three days later, he would rise from death (9:31). Yet the disciples "did not understand what he was saying and were afraid to ask him" (9:32), a lack of response that portrays the disciples (*mathētai*, meaning quite literally "students") as unable to understand what their teacher taught them, not asking him any question, apparently fearful of his rebuke. We will see several other passages in which the disciples of Jesus fail to understand him. Instead of asking their teacher for clarification, these students decide that their remaining in ignorance is better for them. Their decision does not bode well for the future of Jesus and his mission.

Greatness (9:33–37)

This passage seems to be related to other passages in Mark, as well as Matthew and Luke, that show the disciples in personal conflict with each other, concerning which of them was the greatest. It is not hard to see how any group of a dozen people would have such conflicts, but it seems a bit jarring when we realize that this group of a dozen people were the people who would be responsible for conveying the message of Jesus to the world after his death and resurrection. How could it be possible that Jesus, whose life and work were characterized by humility and self-sacrificing service, would be represented by people some of whom seemed to lack humility? The attitude of Jesus's disciples should be, as Mark presents it, the desirable attitude of a child when around adults, namely, being respectful and willing to listen. The actual behavior of the disciples, even among themselves, who are equal in status, appears to be quite the opposite of what Jesus desires it to be. If any of them believe that one of their number is somehow greater than the rest, they believe in something that is not said in the Gospel of

Mark. Matthew 16:17–19 does, of course, envision Peter as the chief of the apostles. *Petros* (Peter) is the *petra* (rock) on which Jesus will build his church (Matt 16:18). This is a clear instance of the profound editing which the Gospel of Matthew does on the Gospel of Mark.

Yet Mark takes Jesus's illustration of his point about humility one step further. Those who will welcome the very humblest people in Jesus's name will not only welcome Jesus himself[4] but will actually welcome the one who sent Jesus, namely, God the Father. Mark thus presents Jesus as teaching, using a little child, the overarching value of humility for his apostles, and by extension, for all of Jesus's followers.

Another Exorcist (9:38–41)

This is an interesting, though short, passage. It illustrates two ideas. First, it shows at least the possibility that there were those not associated with Jesus's actual disciples who would try to use the name of Jesus in a magical way to cast out demons or to do some other deed of power. Second, it shows Jesus as basically tolerant of those who followed him, whom he did not call as apostles or disciples.

Warnings Concerning Temptations (9:42–50)

The warnings in this passage are based on what is known as "eschatological reversal," which is the idea that the ways things are in the present life are the reverse of the ways they will be in the life to come.[5] It is clear to most readers of the Synoptic Gospels that eschatological reversal is characteristic of the teaching of Jesus. Jesus was an eschatological thinker and teacher. Jesus taught that God's kingdom, which was partially present in Jesus's own person, teachings, and deeds of power, would be fully present in the future in a time and in a way that God would choose. In the Lord's Prayer, which we know from Matthew and Luke (but not in Mark or John), there is the famous petition addressed to God, "May your kingdom come" (Matt 6:10; Luke 11:2), which presupposes that God's kingdom is not fully present at the time of Jesus's ministry. The disciples are to pray that God's kingdom will come, and that it will become as present on earth as it is already present

---

4. Compare Matt 25:35–40.
5. *Eschatos* is the Greek adjective for "last." It is the opposite of *prōtos*, "first."

in heaven (Matt 6:10). Thus, the Lord's Prayer, independently of the Gospel of Mark, also presupposes that there is a strongly "not yet" character to God's kingdom. As Jesus taught, when God's kingdom does fully come, there will be massive differences from the ways life is lived now.

Concerning Marriage and Divorce (10:1–12)

Jesus's ministry of preaching, teaching, and healing, not to mention praying, must have taken a great deal of energy, and it is easy to believe that Jesus would want to take some time off from his ministry now and then. If he was not physically tired, he may well have been spiritually exhausted at times. Or, on the other hand, Jesus may have wanted to encounter specifically people who were in "the hill country of Judea and around the Jordan" (10:10). Both explanations are plausible. When he encountered people in these out-of-the-way places, he taught them.

Yet the increasingly organized opposition to Jesus found him and asked him questions designed to make him unpopular ("to test him") with some of the people he was trying to reach. The question asked by the Pharisees was whether it is allowed for a man in good standing in the Jewish community to divorce his wife (10:2). This was an important and serious question since divorce was allowed in the Torah in Deut 24:1–4 and had become part of Jewish tradition. Jesus, however, criticized this tradition, saying that it was "because of your hard-heartedness that Moses wrote this command" (10:5 my trans.). Jesus countered the fact that divorce was allowed in the fifth book of the Torah by arguing from the first book of the Torah, prefacing his argument that it was "from the beginning" (namely, in both of the two creation stories: Gen 1:1—2:4a and Gen 2:4b—3:24) that God had created people male and female (Mark 10:5), and that a man "leaves his father and mother and clings to his wife, and the two shall be one flesh" (Gen 2:24 my trans.). Jesus's judgment on the results of a husband and wife being joined together was, "let no human being separate" (10:9 my trans.). This means that, in the Gospel of Mark, marriage was believed to be indissoluble except by death of one of the spouses.[6]

It is important to note that Matt 19:1–9 edits the passage to allow for divorce if adultery is the cause of the marital breakdown (Matt 19:9). Quite interesting is the fact that this passage cannot be found in Luke at all. This

---

6. For further theological discussion of this passage as part of the New Testament canon, see especially Donfried, *Who Owns the Bible?*, 141–42.

suggests that at least in the matter of divorce the Gospel of Mark was believed by the authors of Matthew and Luke to be too radical.

Those of us who know and care about the many people who have had one or more divorces must be or become interested in why Jesus, according to the Gospel of Mark condemned divorce. The answer is not hard to imagine. Women, both young and old, were generally in vulnerable positions in the ancient world. Jesus stated privately to his disciples that those men who divorced their wives and married another woman according to the legal justification in the Torah would be committing adultery against their original wife, and a woman who divorced her husband and married another man committed adultery against her original husband (10:10–12). This teaching in the Gospel of Mark has led traditionally to the teaching in various Christian traditions of the understanding that marriages, once entered into, cannot be ended by divorce. Although this teaching was understood and meant to uphold the sanctity of marriage, clergy and marriage counselors, along with many other people, know that it is better for either or both spouses that some marriages end. Both the exception for adultery in Matthew and the clear omission of this Markan passage by the Gospel of Luke witness to the fact that the absolute prohibition on divorce in Mark 10:2–12 has been an extremely hard teaching for some to accept, whether in the ancient or contemporary church. In defense of the absolute prohibition on divorce, one can say that in the modern and postmodern world our governments have made it too easy to divorce (and perhaps too easy to get married). In Jesus's time, of course, most marriages were arranged, and they were frequently not based on love but based on the hoped-for stability of families, including the land that families would own. Thus, any reasonable interpretation of Mark 10:2–12 or of Matt 19:3–12 dealing with the issue of divorce—or any New Testament injunction dealing with marriage in any way—should take into account the social differences between the first century CE and our century. The fact that Matthew could and did quite intentionally modify Mark's teaching on divorce, and that Luke in a still more radical editorial move decided to omit it entirely, should give us pause before we decide to enforce Mark 10:10–12 on married people who, for whatever reason, are in unhappy or abusive marriages.

Blessing the Children (10:13-16)

This passage appears to have two parts. First, there is the story of people bringing their children to Jesus so that he might lay his hands on them and bless them. Notably, what happened when people came with their children, seeking Jesus's blessing on them, was that the disciples rebuked those parents (10:13). Jesus "was indignant" at his disciples for their refusal to allow the children to come to him (10:14). Thus, in this passage of only four verses, the Gospel of Mark tells its readers that the disciples of Jesus, apparently—including his inner circle of Peter, James, and John—had the opposite attitude towards children from that of Jesus. The second part of this passage is the exhortation to the readers about how they are to receive the kingdom of God: like little children (10:15). Receiving the kingdom of God like little children who receive a gift seems to be exactly what the adult disciples of Jesus were not interested in doing. They were interested in exerting their authority over others, including other disciples who were, in fact, their peers.

Encounter with the Rich Young Man (10:17-22)

This story begins with a rich young man who runs up to talk to Jesus. Kneeling before Jesus, he addresses Jesus in a flattering way: "Good teacher" (10:17). This form of address is not hard to understand, because as Greek and Roman rhetoric taught, it was first necessary to gain the goodwill of the person or persons listening to a persuasive speech. This was one of the main functions of the *exordium* (Latin) or the *proöimion* (Greek) in rhetorical speeches. The idea was that if the speaker does not gain the goodwill of the audience at the beginning, they will not listen to the rest of it. Jesus refuses to cooperate with this rich man's attempt at persuasion, even in such a trivial matter as his initial address to Jesus as "Good teacher." Jesus challenges the young man, saying that "nobody is good except God alone" (10:18, my trans.). And then Jesus asks questions, like a Torah teacher and, for that matter, not unlike a philosophical teacher. Jesus quotes five of the Ten Commandments, adding "do not defraud" (10:19 my trans.). These questions seem to make little or no impression on the rich young man, who says that he has observed these commands since he was a child (10:20). The young man is described as "rich," and this suggests that he had enough financial means and enough free time to study the Torah, including and especially the Ten Commandments. Mark's readers might think at this point that the man's admission that he had observed the Commandments would be enough for Jesus to enter into a respectful dialogue about their meanings. But Jesus does no such thing. Jesus sees not only the observance of the Ten Commandments as crucial to Torah obedience; he also sees other commands and precepts of Torah as important—deeply important for this rich young man, whose question is how he can receive eternal life (10:17). Jesus, as he looked at the young man, "loved him," which evidently means that he wanted the best for this person, rather than that Jesus felt or expressed romantic or sexual love toward him (10:21).

Jesus asks the rich young man to become one of his disciples: "Come, follow me." A condition of becoming one of Jesus's collaborators was that he had to leave behind his earthly possessions, selling them and then giving the money raised to the poor. By ridding himself of earthly possessions, the young man would have "treasure in heaven" (10:21). Jesus did not advise this renunciation of possessions for everybody that would eventually become members of Jesus-believing congregations, but for his disciples, the original twelve, being free to travel around at Jesus's will was necessary. His disciples were not to be encumbered with possessions, even money, except to buy food to feed people. Except for the purpose of providing support for the poor, the disciples had no need of money or anything money could buy. Thus in Jesus's belief, money would have been unhelpful to his few disciples. They were to be as poor and homeless as he was. This was their calling during the last few years of Jesus's life. After Jesus's death and resurrection, apparently their calling would not have been very different. A full commitment by all of Jesus's disciples was necessary for the success of his mission. The rich young man was unable to give a full commitment to Jesus's mission, and though he was attracted to Jesus's ministry, he was unable to join Jesus and his disciples in it, due to his "many possessions." Thus he went away and was "pained" (10:22).

The Rewards of Discipleship (10:23–31)

The perspective of Jesus's and his disciples' radical renunciation of possessions, which is explicit in the dialogue with the rich young man in 10:17–22, is expanded in this passage, where the renunciation of wealth is not just a requirement for the rich young man (a requirement he refused to comply with) but for all the followers of Jesus, including of course for the first-century readers of Mark. Twenty-first-century readers of Mark may very legitimately ask whether the late first-century readers of Mark really thought they had to give up everything and everybody they loved in order to become followers of Jesus. The historical question, however, is not whether followers of Jesus were willing and ready to give up everything and everybody, but whether this passage has its roots in a saying of Jesus. My view is that there is nothing in this passage that appears particularly unlikely to have come from the historical Jesus.[7] The only question I have about the composition of 10:17–31 concerns the pronouncement in v. 31: "But many who are first will be last, and the last will be first." This saying appears in other contexts in Mark 9:35, in the Epistle of Barnabas 6:13, and in the Oxyrhynchus Papyri 654, 21–27.[8] This saying looks like it could have arisen in any of a number of settings in Jesus's lifetime, and in Mark 10:31 it appears to be an add-on. It illustrates what is usually called "eschatological reversal," the idea that virtually all aspects of the present life will be reversed in the life to come. Those who occupy a high position in society in the present life will be in a much lower position in the next life. Perhaps more importantly, those who occupy a humble position in the present life will be exalted in the life to come. The reversal of positions between this life and the next life is symbolic of how different the kingdom of God will be, when it fully comes, from the life we live now. So Jesus's sayings about eschatological reversal presuppose a radical break between how things are now versus how things will be in the life to come. The existence of Jesus-sayings that speak of reversal in the life to come shows the strong historical likelihood that Jesus was an eschatological thinker and teacher. The coming of the kingdom of God would not be merely an improvement over the present life: it would be a reversal of it. It would be a divine intervention, not merely a set of human reforms. This is what is meant in the Lord's Prayer by the petitions "your kingdom come, your will be done, on earth as it is in heaven." God's perfect will is already being done in heaven, and those who pray the Lord's Prayer ask that God cause God's will to be done on earth where believers are now.

A significantly difficult part of this passage is 10:25, the famous verse in which Jesus states that it would be "easier for a camel to pass through the

---

7. Taylor, *Gospel According to St. Mark*, 430: "There can be little doubt that the story rests on authentic tradition, ultimately that of an eyewitness, for it is lifelike." Of course, it may be said that this comment by Taylor is far from earth-shaking in light of his usual position against some conclusions of form criticism.

8. These references come from Kurt Aland, *Synopsis Quattuor Evangeliorum*, §255.

eye of a needle than for a rich person to enter the kingdom of God" (my trans.). This verse has been the subject of much misinterpretation, consisting of the theory of the existence of a gate in the city wall of Jerusalem called "the eye of the needle." Such a gate did not exist, despite many sermons having been preached on it. The proposed existence of a gate in the city wall through which a camel could actually pass is nothing less than an attempt to make the saying of Jesus in 10:25 considerably less radical and stringent than it is. Instead of making it impossible for the rich to enter the kingdom of God, the camel's actually being able to pass through "the eye of a needle" suggests that it is quite possible for the rich to enter the kingdom of God. The rhetorical power of this famous pronouncement is contained in the obvious impossibility of a large beast of burden's going through a needle's eye.

The Third Prediction of the Passion (10:32–34)

The first prediction of the passion, death, and resurrection was quite eventful. Peter contradicted what Jesus said about his suffering and death, and for that, Jesus addressed him as "Satan" (8:32–33), since Peter's opposition to Jesus's prediction of the passion was quite the opposite of what Jesus said about himself. To directly contradict Jesus, especially on the matter of what would be happening to him, was to support what the powers of evil wanted, not what God had in mind. This third prediction of the passion met with silence from the apostles, despite the fact that "they were amazed, and those who followed were afraid" (10:32). It was nonetheless Jesus's will to go to Jerusalem. It clearly appears that Jesus knew that his time in Jerusalem would be dangerous for himself, if not also for his apostles. This little passage, with the third statement of Jesus's prediction of his passion, death, and resurrection from death, emphasizes one more time the centrality of the fate of Jesus. His suffering and death at the hands of the Roman occupation government are at the heart of how Jesus is presented in the Gospel of Mark. Instead of politely or diplomatically avoiding any discussion of Jesus's degrading suffering and death, Mark emphasizes them. And Mark emphasizes how unprepared the disciples are for Jesus's suffering and death, not to mention for the likelihood of their own suffering and martyrdom in the years to come. By the time the Gospel of Mark was written and being copied, and thus preserved, the martyrdoms of followers of Jesus were quite real. The later the dates for the composition, copying, and distribution of Mark, the more prominent the issue of the martyrdoms of Jesus-followers is.

Rank Among the Disciples (10:35–45)

As if to emphasize how unprepared the disciples are for their own personal suffering, the two sons of Zebedee, who were the third and fourth apostles to be called by Jesus (1:19–20), initiate a conversation with Jesus in order to ask for the top positions in Jesus's coming kingdom. This passage shows that even two of the four earliest disciples of Jesus, precisely after having heard the teaching and preaching of Jesus for several months, do not understand the central message of the Gospel of Mark about suffering: they comprehend neither Jesus's imminent suffering nor their own. James and John are quite content to be followers of Jesus, provided their service as apostles will lead to earthly glory or at least recognition as the two top leaders within the community of Jesus-believers. The top position, other than Jesus's position, was the position for the one who would sit "at your right hand . . . in your glory" (10:37). The next person in order of leadership would be the one sitting at Jesus's left hand. Their cheeky request shows a lack of understanding of what the role of an apostle should be in the church. At least early readers of Mark understood how inappropriate James and John's request was, so that it is the mother of James and John, instead of James and John themselves, who makes this request in Matt 20:20, while Luke omits this passage entirely.[9] This passage, and what it says about two of the inner-circle of apostles, has to be added to the long list of passages that can very reasonably be understood to show the apostles in an unfavorable light.

The Healing of Bartimaeus (10:46–52)

This section of Mark is rounded out by a healing miracle, the healing of a blind man. The blind man has an Aramaic name, Bartimaeus, which means "son of Timaeus." This miracle story is not an exorcism but does feature the usual elements of a healing miracle. There is a dialogue between the blind man and bystanders, in which the bystanders tell the blind man to be silent, to which the blind man responds by shouting still louder. In his shouts he

---

9. Aland, *Synopsis of the Four Gospels*, §263.

addresses Jesus as "Son of David" (10:47–48). Jesus asks the bystanders to call him so that Jesus can speak with him (10:49). The blind man tells Jesus that he wants to see, and Jesus heals him, saying, "Your faith has saved you" (10:52). The emphasis in this miracle story is not the driving out of an evil spirit but the healing of a man who had faith in Jesus.

8

Jesus in Jerusalem
Mark 11:1—13:37

THIS SECTION OF MARK begins with Jesus's entry into Jerusalem, and it narrates his activity in Jerusalem, up to but not including the passion narrative, which is the long and dramatic text describing the suffering and death of Jesus in chapters 14 and 15. Chapter 13 of Mark includes an apocalyptic discourse, detailing a timetable for the events before and during the coming of the Son of Man.

Jesus's "Triumphal Entry" (11:1-10)

The traditional title for this passage, "the triumphal entry," causes readers of Mark to ask the question, Just what kind of entrance did Jesus make into Jerusalem? In the context of the ancient world, it doesn't seem in the least triumphal. Jesus's entry into Jerusalem, riding a colt, is appropriate to the fact that Jesus did not come celebrating a military victory. He did not come as a person whose power over other people was being celebrated. One could argue that it was a ride into Jerusalem that was humble rather than triumphal or triumphant. Yet as Jesus was riding into the city, people started crying out these shouts of acclamation: "Hosanna! Blessed is the one who comes in the name of the Lord! Blessed is the coming kingdom of our ancestor David! Hosanna in the highest heaven!" These shouts of acclamation have very strong messianic associations. Jesus was not referred to as a son of David, yet the "coming kingdom of our ancestor David" clearly refers to a kingdom that was different from the Roman Empire. The kingdom in this set of acclamations meant a restored Israel with a new king who would be in the line of David. Of course, a restored Israel with a new Davidic king would be in great opposition to the Roman order enforced both before and after the Jewish War of 66–70 CE.

In his excellent book, Joachim Gnilka points out the messianic and thus political significance of the acclamations by those fellow pilgrims who were present at Jesus's entry into Jerusalem, as Mark presents it. First of all, the sending of disciples to find, untie, and bring a colt for Jesus to ride into Jerusalem was providential (11:2–6). Jesus's riding the colt, on which had been laid various cloaks, together with the cloaks and leafy branches brought from the fields and laid on the road, recalls for Mark's readers Zech 9:9, in which the prophet foresaw the advent of a king who would bring peace: "Rejoice greatly, O daughter Zion! Shout aloud, O daughter Jerusalem! Lo, your king comes to you, triumphant and victorious is he, humble and riding on a donkey, on a colt, the foal of a donkey." The king prophesied by Zechariah does not lead a military procession by riding a warhorse, but comes humbly, riding a donkey or a colt. Yet the king who comes to Jerusalem in Zechariah's poetry is fully consistent with the Lord's victory over the powers which have threatened Israel's existence as a nation. Thus, the symbolic entry of the new king into Jerusalem, after the Lord subdues the enemies of Israel, had everything to do with the prophecy of a messianic king whose power comes from God, who will give the new king of Israel victory over the other invading nations of the ancient Near East. Of this king, Zechariah continues: "He will cut off the chariot from Ephraim and the warhorse from Jerusalem; and the battle bow shall be cut off, and he shall command peace to the nations; his dominion shall be from sea to sea, and from the River to the ends of the earth . . . On that day the LORD their God will save them for they are the flock of his people; for like the jewels of a crown they shall shine on his land" (Zech 9:10, 16). So the Old Testament text or texts standing behind Mark 11:7–10 pointed the readers to the prospect of God's victory over the enemies of the people of God, and to the establishment of a renewed Israel, after a bloody war, in peace. This is what was meant by a "messianic age": the perennial geopolitical problems experienced in its ancient Near Eastern setting by Israel would be finally resolved by Israel's military might, which would come from none other than the God of Israel.

There was a deep symbolic meaning in the "triumphal entry" of Jesus into Jerusalem for Jews who were aware of the prophecy of Zechariah, and for the readers of Mark, within the context of Second Temple Judaism. Similarly, we must ask how the Roman governing establishment would have viewed Jesus's symbolic entry into the capital city, in which it has been estimated that in addition to its 55,000 residents, there were 125,000 pilgrims at the time of Passover.[1] From the standpoint of the Roman governor of Judaea, Jerusalem at Passover may well have seemed like a powder keg which might well explode with any provocation. Thus, because of the high population of Jews from both Jerusalem and the Diaspora at or near the festival of Passover, the Roman governor was highly motivated to "keep the lid on things" and avoid fomenting or contributing to a riot. The leadership of Judaism in Jerusalem would have been equally motivated to avoid a riot, which would have resulted in many Jewish deaths.

So, the highly symbolic entry of Jesus into Jerusalem was both political and dangerous. This was perhaps not so much because of what Jesus was doing as because of what Jesus's fellow pilgrims in Jerusalem did in acclaiming him in ways that suggested he was making a kingly entry into the holy city. The politics, of course, had nothing to do with modern partisan politics but had everything to do with the precarious position of the Jewish community as a large group of people strongly oppressed by the Roman occupation government. That so many of the Jews in Jerusalem at Passover were not residents of the holy city meant that the gathering of Jews in Jerusalem was both large and unstable. The instability of the Passover pilgrims within the Roman imperial context made for danger. To my mind, it is unthinkable that Jesus of Nazareth would not have known about this danger.

Jesus in Jerusalem (11:11)

As a devout Jew, it makes perfect sense for Jesus to have wanted to see the temple in Jerusalem, especially since, according to Mark, Matthew, and Luke, Jesus only went to Jerusalem once as an adult. We will read in 11:15–17 of Jesus's extended encounter in the temple.

---

1. Gnilka, *Jesus of Nazareth*, 272.

The Fig Tree and Its Fate (11:12–14, 20–26)

Traditionally, most liberal interpreters of the Gospels have significant difficulty with this passage. Jesus was hungry, so he went to pick a fig to eat, and the problem was that there was no fig on the tree, since figs were not in season at that time. They had not yet had a chance to grow. And so, unexpectedly, Jesus cursed the fig tree by saying, "May no one ever eat fruit from you again" (11:14). One might wonder why Jesus cursed an innocent fig tree that, in fact, he did not own or for which he had no responsibility. This would be the wrong question. In the context of the life of Jesus, miracle stories were told and collected because of what they conveyed to believers about imitating Jesus's way of life and especially about the power of Jesus. Of course, the fact that Jesus was hungry (11:12) illustrates the humanity of Jesus. And, even more strongly, this miracle story shows the power of Jesus, as we read in 11:20–26. After the fig tree is cursed in 11:14, Jesus and his disciples return to it the next morning and see that it has withered. So, however one may evaluate the morality of Jesus's cursing the out-of-season fig tree when he did, this miracle story illustrates both the human nature of Jesus and also the fact that during his earthly life, he was able to do miracles. The withering of the fig tree by the morning after its cursing by Jesus shows the reader one more example of Jesus's ability to do deeds of power, quite apart from the much more frequent miracles of healing.

Another interpretation of the cursing of the fig tree is that the fig tree was symbolic of God's planting of Israel, which calls to mind the song of the vineyard in Isaiah 5:1–7. The unproductivity of the vineyard in Isaiah's song was an agricultural metaphor for the disobedience and sinfulness of Israel. In the song of the vineyard, the fact that the vineyard only produced wild grapes instead of the desired grapes (which actually God had planted), meant that God would "remove its hedge, and it shall be devoured; I will break down its wall, and it shall be trampled down" (Isa 5:5). So the cursing of the unproductive fig tree is analogous to the removal of divine protection from Israel, sung about in Isa 5:5–6. It is consistent with the coming war between Jewish rebels and the Roman occupation forces.

The "Cleansing" of the Temple (11:15–17)

More provocative than Jesus's entry into Jerusalem in 11:1–11 was the so-called cleansing of the temple. The so-called triumphal entry was likely to attract the notice of the Roman occupation government because of the royal overtones to the messianic acclamations which greeted Jesus upon entering Jerusalem. The cleansing of the temple would have been more provocative to the Jewish hierarchy in Jerusalem than the triumphal entry, since they were the authorities that governed the temple precincts.

The "cleansing" of the temple, as it is called, means its purification from the making of money by those who were taking advantage of those pilgrims who came to the temple to have animal sacrifices offered for themselves by the priests. The money changers were those who would take Roman coins from pilgrims and exchange them for temple coinage, which did not bear the image of the Roman emperor. Of course, we are not told what the exchange rates were, yet it seems very likely that the rates were not favorable to the religious pilgrims visiting Jerusalem. There were also animals that were sold in the temple precincts to pilgrims, so that visitors could have these animals offered in sacrifice. Again, it is not hard to imagine that the prices of these animals were elevated, since pilgrims to Jerusalem would bring with them not sacrificial animals but money. Although it was necessary to have coins available to be used to buy offerings in the temple, as well as animals available for sacrifice, it is not easy to discern why Jesus would object to these items, which were necessary for the temple cult, except if Jesus opposed price gouging, about which we are not told in the text of Mark.[2] Country and small-town people like Jesus and his disciples might very well have found this commerce appalling and quite the opposite of what should have taken place in the temple, even in the court of the Gentiles.

Conspiracy Against Jesus (11:18-19)

This demonstration in the temple could not possibly have gone unnoticed by the hierarchy of Judaism in Jerusalem. Not surprisingly, "the chief priests and the scribes" were afraid of Jesus, "because the whole crowd was spellbound by his teaching" (11:18). Thus, it is historically credible that they would be motivated to attempt to remove Jesus and his movement, even by killing him, not least because they feared that any uprising by Jews in Jerusalem at Passover would tempt the Roman occupation forces to put down any Jewish insurrection by bloody force. Ironically, the more popular Jesus was, the more danger there was for the Jewish community from the

---

2. In favor of the interpretation that the merchants and moneychangers in the temple precincts were price gouging, see Taylor, *Gospel According to St. Mark*, 463.

Roman occupation forces. As it got darker, Jesus and company exited the city. This exit would have made it possible one more time for Jesus to flee to Galilee and stay out of trouble, at least relatively speaking. Jesus did not choose to do that.

Jesus's Authority (11:27–33)

The conflict between Jesus on the one hand and "the chief priests, the scribes, and the elders" on the other hand (11:27) now accelerates. The day after Jesus has forcibly cleared the merchants out of the temple, the Jewish authorities confront him in the temple precincts, asking by what authority Jesus does the things he does. This, of course, is a perfectly germane question for these leaders to ask Jesus. The question itself shows first of all that they recognize how different Jesus's approach to Jewish religious life is from theirs. It is a hostile question, to be sure, because the very asking of this question presupposes that the questioners do not think that Jesus has the authority to act as he does. Their question is nothing less than the opening salvo in their rhetorical attempt to refute Jesus. They are trying to get him to commit what they would have called blasphemy, if he had said he was the Son of God or a prophet or some other religious figure that the Jerusalem hierarchy was quite unprepared to authorize. If he had not claimed to be Son of God or some other exalted religious figure, then they would have used his answer to smear him by saying, "See, this pretender has no authority from God or anybody else." Thus, their question was loaded. Answering it was dangerous—and Jesus clearly knew it. So Jesus, like any number of rabbis, answered a question with a question. In this case, Jesus's question to the Jerusalem hierarchy was equally loaded. He asks whether the baptism of John the Baptizer was "from heaven, or was it of human origin?" (11:30). This one question was as dangerous to the Jewish leadership as their question to Jesus had been. The Jewish questioners of Jesus did not want to be put in a situation where they condemned John the Baptizer, since he was so popular. If they were to say that John's baptism was "from heaven" (meaning "from God"), then Jesus would counter with another, even more provocative, question: "Why then did you not believe him?" (11:31). So neither Jesus nor his Jewish questioners answered each other's question, because any answer that either of them gave would have given the other debating points in the future. In order to avoid being refuted or being thought to be blasphemous, silence was the better option for both Jesus and the

Jewish leaders who questioned him in the temple precincts. Even though this interaction ended in a standoff, this passage exhibits a clear heightening of the conflict between Jesus and the Jerusalem hierarchy.

The Parable of the Crooked Sharecroppers (12:1–12)

This parable, which could be called the parable of the vineyard or the parable of the crooked sharecroppers, has parallels in Matt 21:33–46 and Luke 20:9–19. This story has Isa 5:1–7, the song of the vineyard, in the background. As mentioned before, the song of the vineyard, which was poetry (and was therefore a song) by Isaiah dealt with God's relationship with Israel. Instead of the vineyard yielding good grapes, the vineyard yielded only wild grapes, which were good for neither eating nor making wine. The meaning of the song of the vineyard was that Israel did not meet God's expectations when he established and protected Israel from its enemies in the ancient Near East. Without God's protection, Israel could not stand against its enemies. Thus, the Assyrian invasion happened in the northern kingdom and the Babylonian captivity happened in the southern kingdom. As a result, the vineyard—meaning Israel—was trampled down and destroyed. Hence the song of the vineyard was a prophetic warning to Israel and a call to the divided monarchy to be faithful to the God of Israel. This prophetic warning was not heeded.

In our passage in Mark, the parable of the wicked husbandmen is also a warning to those who are put in charge of the vineyard. In this parable, the vineyard stands for God's creation of the world, and those who are put in charge of the vineyard are those who inhabit the world who claim to be believers in God, most likely those who are Jews. The grape growers grow their grapes, and they do bring in a good harvest of grapes. By the agreement they made with the vineyard owner, who stands for God, the owner has the legal right to receive his share of either the harvested grapes or of the wine they produce. The problem is that the evil sharecroppers refuse to pay their share of the grapes or wine to the vineyard owner. The legality of the agreement between the owner and the sharecroppers is, in point of fact, the law of Moses. By refusing to give the vineyard owner what he is owed, the evil sharecroppers are, in contemporary terms, perpetrating fraud. Thus, the workers in the vineyard, who stand for the people of ancient Israel who did not do as God commanded and as they probably had agreed to do in Israelite or Jewish liturgical ceremonies, are people who may have proudly claimed their religious heritage, but they refused to practice it. They claimed to be part of Israel, they lived in God's creation, and they reaped the benefits of God's creation, but then they did not do their part in keeping any covenant. That is what it meant for the crooked sharecroppers to keep the owner's share of the produce. Then when the owner sends his servants—who stand for the prophets—to collect the produce, the crooked sharecroppers beat up several of them and even kill one. Then the owner decides to send his own "beloved son" (12:6). In fact, they kill the son of the owner and even entertain the idea that someday the vineyard will belong to them (12:7). The owner's just response is to come and "destroy the tenants and give the vineyard to others" (12:9).

It does appear that the son of the owner stands for the Son of God, Jesus. The fact that this parable has both the owner's sending his son and the owner's son being put to death suggests that the identifications of God with the vineyard owner and of Jesus with the vineyard owner's son who is sent and is put to death by the crooked sharecroppers should be central to the interpretation of this parable. If this parable did originate from the historical Jesus, it is one more confirmation of Jesus's understanding of his own role and of his impending death. It would confirm for Mark's readers yet one more time the voluntary nature of Jesus's self-sacrifice, because Jesus knew that he was the human counterpart of the owner's son in the parable, whom the vineyard owner sent and whom the evil sharecroppers would put to an unjust death.

This parable also illustrates eschatological reversal, which is the concept that things in the present life are reversed from the way they will be in the life to come. The epitome of this concept in this parable is the biblical quote from Ps 118:22–23 in Mark 12:10–11. The one who was rejected at first, namely, Jesus, will become the cornerstone in the life to come. This bit of biblical rhetoric caused the Jewish leaders, who had accosted Jesus in 11:27–32 and had been controverted by Jesus's clever rejoinder in 11:33, to walk away from Jesus in 12:12: "they wanted to arrest him, but they feared the crowd. So they left him and went away." Even more telling is Mark's comment in the same verse that "they realized that he had told this parable against them." So Jesus silenced the top leaders of the Jewish community in Jerusalem with a parable that he told "against them." This was a rhetorical victory, at least for the moment.

Paying Tribute to Caesar? (12:13–17)

The top Jewish leaders, having been silenced by Jesus, now send "some Pharisees and some Herodians to trap him in what he said" (12:13). The purpose of sending Pharisees and Herodians "to trap him in what he said" reveals the failure of the "chief priests, the scribes, and the elders" to score a rhetorical victory over Jesus in 11:27–33. They then send in people rather more skilled in rhetorical attack than themselves. The Pharisees and Herodians ask Jesus a question that was not designed to get Jesus in trouble with Jewish authorities, as the previous encounter had been, but a question carefully crafted to get Jesus in trouble with the Roman authorities, since it dealt with whether or not it was appropriate for Jews to pay taxes. If Jesus had said it was not lawful, according to the Torah, to pay taxes to the Roman emperor, he would have been sent by the Herodians quite directly to some government official to be charged. If he had said it was in accordance with the Torah to pay Roman taxes, the Pharisees could well have disputed this, since the Roman emperor was a pagan ruler, actually a ruler of a foreign country. For Jews strictly adhering to biblical tradition, the only king is God. Those Jews who acted as tax collectors were collaborators with the Roman oppressors, and they were often shunned. Jesus gave an answer that could have been interpreted in several ways: "Give to the emperor the things that are the emperor's, and to God the things that are God's" (12:17). This answer did not advise Jews in the Roman province of Judea not to pay Roman taxes, as the Pharisees and Herodians probably hoped Jesus's reply would do. Importantly, no response from these Jewish interlocutors to Jesus's answer is given in Mark. This means that Jesus silenced them in debate.

The Sadducees' Question About the Resurrection (12:18–27)

Now the Sadducees ask Jesus a question that is clearly designed to trip him up. The Sadducees, according to the New Testament and various Jewish documents, did not believe in the resurrection of the dead.[3] So, their question to Jesus in this passage can only be considered a "trick question," to use a modern phrase. Here, the intent was not to get Jesus in trouble with the Roman authorities but to stir up trouble with the priestly establishment,

---

3. Strack and Billerbeck, *Commentary*, 1:1014–17.

which was populated with Sadducees. The stunning story they weave to try to trip Jesus up is about a woman who had been married sequentially to seven brothers. The question was this: "In the resurrection whose wife will she be? For the seven had the same wife" (12:23). If Jesus were to identify any of the seven brothers to whom the woman had been married, the obvious objection to Jesus's possible answer would be to inquire why one brother and not any of the others should be considered her rightful husband. Obviously the question, as posed in this dialogue with Sadducees, was an attempt to make the resurrection seem like a foolish idea, if not also an adulterous idea. Jesus, of course, would not have denied the reality of the resurrection of the dead, and several groups within Second Temple Judaism would have agreed with him in his affirmation of the afterlife. And so Jesus appealed to some of the oldest traditions within Judaism and the Hebrew religion, actually going back to some of the earliest stories in the Torah, the ancestral narratives. The God of Israel was not just any ancient Near Eastern deity: this deity was none other than "the God of Abraham, the God of Isaac, and the God of Jacob" (Mark 12:26; compare Exod 3:6). This was, quite bluntly, the God the Sadducees believed in and claimed to follow. Jesus's claim that God is not the God of the dead but of the living, as witnessed by God's ancient and traditional titles as "the God of Abraham and the God of Isaac and the God of Jacob" had its origin in the greatest fountain of tradition in Judaism, the Torah of Moses, and specifically in the second book of the Torah, Exodus. Thus, as Jesus reasoned, the Sadducees would not have been able to attack his interpretation of Exodus in Mark 12:26–27 (including his interpretation of God's revelation to Moses himself) without attacking the Torah itself and indeed God's very first words to Moses in Exod 3:4–6. Jesus's last remark to the Sadducees in 12:27, "you are highly mistaken," gives an emphatic conclusion to Jesus's polemical, rhetorical question in 12:24, at the beginning of his answer to them: "Is not this the reason you are wrong, that you know neither the scriptures nor the power of God?" By the end of this passage, in 12:27, Jesus has silenced the chief priests, scribes, Pharisees, Herodians, and Sadducees by successfully answering their trick questions. These hostile Jerusalem interlocutors of Jesus, having heard his answers, are unwilling to respond further by raising objections to his reasoning. Despite their years of education in Torah and Jewish tradition, and irrespective of their political connections with the Roman governing authorities, they are refuted by Jesus, from an obscure town in Galilee.

The Greatest Commandments (12:28–34)

This passage starts out on a more positive note than the previous passages with the hostile dialogues initiated by those who are trying to trip Jesus up. The scribe who approaches Jesus in this passage "heard [Jesus's opponents] disputing with one another, and [saw] that he answered them well" (12:28). He asks Jesus a straightforward question: "Which commandment is the first of all?" (12:28). This question, or questions like it, presupposed that those who interpret the Torah have the ability to discuss and to discern which commands in the Torah were the "first" or "weightiest," meaning the most important. Thus, this question is not a trick question: it is perfectly appropriate and central to the religious understanding and practice of Judaism.

Jesus answers this question from the scribe by quoting scriptures from the Torah. First in importance was the Shemaʻ, which is found in Deut 6:4–5. These famous verses proclaim that God is one, and they also enshrine the command to love God "with your whole heart and with your whole soul and with your whole strength" (Mark 12:29–30 my trans.); Mark also adds "with your whole mind." Then, the second commandment in importance is Lev 19:18, the command to love one's neighbor as much as one loves oneself (Mark 12:31). This command presupposes that the person obeying it loves his or her own life; this command sees that the necessary counterpart to loving one's own life is the love of one's neighbor. The Gospel of Mark sees both of these commands as necessary for followers of Jesus. Being a follower of Jesus is not just a matter of one's eternal salvation in the life to come; it is also about living life with other people here and now. This command from Jesus is not only in the Torah; it is also foundational in the books of the Prophets.

The scribe who had asked Jesus these questions obviously approved of Jesus's answers: he says, "You are right, teacher" (12:32). He then recounts what Jesus's specific answers—taken from Torah—had been, even adding his own comment that to obey the love command "is much more important than all whole burnt offerings and sacrifices" (12:32–33). Jesus "saw that he answered wisely" and then "said to him, 'You are not far from the kingdom of God.'" This supportive response from the scribe, a Scripture expert, in addition to Jesus's own answers, which were quotations from the Torah itself, causes the onlookers to keep silent (12:34). Once more, Jesus silenced people who were in various leadership positions within Judaism in Jerusalem. Very notably, only the scribe, a Scripture scholar to be sure, gives his stamp of approval to what Jesus has said in answer to the scribe's classic and remarkably traditional question about the Bible: "Which commandment is the first of all?" This approval implies that this scribe found Jesus's religious perspective and answers to his biblical question very much within the norms of Jewish belief.

About David's Son (12:35–37a)

Now Jesus turns the tables on most of his questioners. After the approving response from the scribe who had asked him a straightforward Torah question (12:28), Jesus starts asking what could clearly be considered a trick question involving the interpretation of a messianic psalm, actually a psalm for the enthronement of a king of Israel, namely, Ps 110. It is quite a complicated question that Jesus asks in Mark 12:35–37a. It is worth noting that his question was an unanswerable one, unless it is understood that "my Lord" (Mark 12:36; Ps 110:1) is court language used in an address to a king who is being enthroned.

Woes to the Scribes and Pharisees (12:37b–40)

Mark notes that "the large crowd was listening to him with delight" (12:37b). The crowd was happy to hear Jesus now asking questions to confute his previous questioners. Perhaps we are justified in pointing out that the crowd in Jerusalem took pleasure in seeing the country carpenter's son from Nazareth in Galilee putting a question to the elites of the Jerusalem hierarchy that was too difficult for them to answer. The crowd's delight at the Pharisees' and Sadducees', and perhaps the scribes', inability to answer Jesus's question is the only response recorded in Mark to Jesus's trick question in 12:35–37.

The delight of the crowd as they witnessed Jesus's silencing his learned detractors who had tried to trip him up in public debate is in great contrast to what follows. In 12:35–37a Jesus had asked what was frankly a trick question. Now in 12:37b–40 Jesus moves away from a question of technical Torah interpretation to an all-out attack on the scribes. (In the expanded parallel passage in Matt 23:1–36, Jesus attacks not only scribes but also Pharisees.) According to Mark, the scribes not only act in unjust ways on the streets and expect prime synagogue seating and the best places at dinners; they also "devour the homes of widows," even as they are "praying long prayers" (12:40 my trans.). Thus, Jesus attacks the scribes for their outward show of religion, as their display of piety was accompanied by a lack of zeal for the plight of poor widows. Obviously Jesus was in synch with the tradition of the prophets of the Hebrew Bible.

The Widow's Mite (12:41–44)

The mention of widows in 12:40 is followed by the contrast between the contributions to the temple treasury by "many rich people" and "one poor widow" (12:41). The temple treasury was enriched greatly by its wealthy contributors, while the widow only put in two *lepta*, which together made up a *quadrans*. These were small copper coins, and when the two coins were added together, they did not amount to much. Yet Jesus calls his disciples to listen, saying that "this poor widow has contributed much more than all the contributions into the treasury" (12:43 my trans.). Though others gave large amounts, what the poor widow put in was all she had to live on. Thus, in proportion to the large amounts given by rich people, the widow's very small contribution was greater, since it was all she had. This narrative about the poor widow's contribution doesn't make sense in terms of finance, yet it does make sense in terms of the religious value of the contributions to the temple treasury. Jesus raises the standard of giving from offering large sums of money for the temple treasury to giving one's whole life to God.

The Coming Destruction of the Temple (13:1–2)

These two verses are the first verses of the eschatological discourse, one of the two major speeches Jesus gives in Mark. The historical interpretation of these verses is crucial to the dating of the Gospel of Mark. If Jesus said what is in 13:2, that not a single stone will be left on top of another stone, then this means that Jesus did in fact predict the destruction of the Jerusalem temple. If Jesus did not say what is written in Mark 13:2, then this is an instance of *ex eventu* prophecy, also known to scholars as *vaticinium ex eventu*. *Ex eventu* ("out of the event") prophecy is prophecy of an event that has already taken place, which is inserted in a religious or historical text. The purpose of an insertion of this type is to add historical likelihood, sometimes called "verisimilitude," to the text as a whole. On the one hand, there is clear evidence of the existence of *ex eventu* prophecy in several pieces of apocalyptic literature, so it is not unexpected that such prophecy might well be found here in what's sometimes called the Markan

Apocalypse or the Little Apocalypse, of chapter 13. On the other hand, it is not impossible for Jesus to have predicted the destruction of the Jerusalem temple, given the precariousness of Jewish existence in the Roman province called Iudaea. Jesus and his disciples surely knew that a Jewish uprising in Judea would be put down with deadly force by the Romans.[4] Thus, we can say that the Gospel of Mark portrays Jesus as prophesying the destruction of the temple in Jerusalem, without knowing whether this prophecy actually goes back Jesus's own teaching. In the context of Jewish life, however, the destruction of the Jerusalem temple eventually was a terrible blow to all Jews, including to Jesus-believers. The destruction of the temple constituted an extreme form of the persecution of the righteous, a standard topic well known in apocalyptic writings. The temple's destruction signified the withdrawal of God's presence from the center of Jewish religion, which in the minds of Jews who lived through it was likely the greatest disaster of all.

Signs Before the Second Coming (13:3-13)

In this passage, the four original apostles of Jesus ask Jesus privately about the second coming. They want to know for certain when it will happen, and what the signs preceding it will be (13:4). These are not unreasonable questions by any means: believers in God would like to know when God's intervention will be. Often, apocalyptic literature does tell its readers about the signs preceding and accompanying the divine intervention. Jesus responds with a warning against being deceived by false messiahs.

That Jesus-believing groups in the first century were apparently experiencing some persecutions is interpreted in this passage as a sign that the process that would move toward the eventual divine intervention—the coming of the Son of Man—had begun. Cosmic events have not yet happened, but eventually they will (13:24-27). Before the cosmic events happen, there will be "wars and rumors of wars" and various conflicts between and among nations, as well as famines (13:8).

In 13:9-13, there are specific persecutions which will happen. Jesus-believers will be persecuted for their belief, even by fellow Jews (13:9): believers in Jesus will be handed over to "sanhedrins" and "synagogues" (my trans.). Yet even with these persecutions of Jesus-believers by fellow Jews, the gospel "must first be proclaimed to all nations" (13:10). "All nations" is the usual translation of *panta ta ethnē*, quite literally meaning "all the

---

4. Gnilka, *Jesus of Nazareth*, 26-37, as well as Horsley, *Galilee*, 62-185.

Gentiles." Though the persecution by fellow human beings—indeed, fellow Jews—will be severe, endurance by followers of Jesus "to the end" will result in salvation (13:13).

The Abomination (13:14-20)

The desolating sacrilege, traditionally called "the abomination of desolation," is based on passages in the biblical book of Daniel. The sacrilege is referred to in Dan 11:31 and 12:11, and is alluded to in 9:27. In Daniel the sacrilege is a statue depicting a Syrian deity (not the God of Israel) placed in the Jerusalem temple. This passage may reference other sacrileges that appeared closer in time to when the Gospel of Mark was written down and circulated.[5] When the divine intervention happens, says Jesus in Mark's Gospel, it will happen suddenly, with only various signs indicating that the intervention is in process (13:14-16).

Comings of False Messiahs (13:21-23) and the Coming of the Son of Man (13:24-27)

As part of the signs of the coming of the Son of Man, the deception of weaker believers by false messiahs and prophets will take place (13:21-22). Signs of the cosmos being changed and shaken will occur, with changes in sun, moon, and stars (13:24-25). These cosmic signs will be followed by the greatest cosmic sign of all: the coming of the Son of Man. The angels in the heavens will gather the elect from all over the cosmos (13:26-27).

The Parable of the Fig Tree (13:28-32)

A fig tree that has already been the recipient of a miracle in 11:12-14 and 11:20-21 conveys a symbolic meaning here. The basic idea is that fig trees produce leaves and eventually figs that ripen, and they do these things on their own schedule. In the cursing of the fig tree in Mark 11, the importance of the fig tree is that it is supposed to be productive—to produce figs that will eventually ripen. The fig tree cursed in Mark 11 is symbolic of unproductive Israel, in Jesus's view. Here in chapter 13, the import of the fig tree is different: The fig is a fruit on a tree that, unless the fruit is spoiled

---

5. Marcus, *Mark 8-16*, 889-91.

in some way, will inexorably produce ripe, sweet figs that will be good to harvest and to eat. The appearance of leaves on a fig tree is a certain forecast that "summer is near" (13:28). The appearance of leaves reminds those who are interested in harvesting figs that winter is over and summer is on the way. Thus, the readers of Mark are to understand that the signs before the coming of the Son of Man make it certain that the Son of Man is coming as judge and redeemer, to gather the followers of Jesus from the ends of the earth and the ends of heaven. Then after the Jesus-believers are gathered by the angels, they will enter a place of eternal safety and bliss. This eternal safety and bliss, of course, is the opposite of what many Jesus-believers were experiencing at the time of the writing of Mark. Jesus's words are eternal, even though heaven and earth are not (13:31). When will these cosmic events take place? The Gospel of Mark does not tell its readers: neither Jesus himself nor the heavenly angels know. Only God the Father knows (13:32).

Conclusion to the Eschatological Speech (13:33–37)

The lengthy eschatological speech by Jesus, and Jesus's activity in Jerusalem before his passion and death, now comes to an end at 13:37. Although no believers in Jesus know when the Son of Man will come, that does not mean that there should be any doubt that Jesus is making his second coming. Thus, even though it will be a long time (and obviously the writer of Mark did not know that it would be some two thousand years or more) before Jesus comes back, believers in Jesus, even though persecuted either by secular governments or by various members of the Jewish hierarchy or in local synagogues, must not grow weary or fall asleep (13:35–37).

9

The Passion of Jesus
Mark 14:1—15:47

THIS SECTION OF MARK is the "passion narrative." It tells of the suffering and death of Jesus. It is the necessary prelude to the resurrection in chapter 16. The fact that the disciples saw the suffering and death of Jesus helps to explain their lack of belief in his resurrection. Martin Kähler is famous for his statement that the Gospels are "passion narratives with extended introductions."[1] Whereas Mark was content to summarize the teaching and healing activity of Jesus in various places, there is a major increase in the level of detail from chapter 14 onward. Some scholars have thought that this meant that there was a preexisting passion narrative that the writer of Mark used and inserted in this gospel.

The Planning of Jesus's Death (14:1–2)

The history of any event surely includes its prehistory. We have seen previously in Mark a growing level of tension between Jesus and the Jewish hierarchy in Jerusalem, including scribes, Pharisees, Sadducees (members of the priestly class and collaborators with the Roman occupation government), and elders. The "chief priests and the scribes" had decided to eliminate Jesus, and they knew the only way he could be put to death was if the Roman government did it. Thus, while they wanted to have Jesus arrested,

---

1. Kähler, *So-Called Historical Jesus*, 80n11.

they did not want to start a riot. This strongly suggests that these Jewish leaders knew that Jesus was popular, perhaps not only among pilgrims to Jerusalem who were from Galilee.

Jesus's Anointing in Bethany (14:3-9)

Also in anticipation of Jesus's death is the episode of the anointing of Jesus's head by the unnamed woman in Bethany. This story has attracted attention because of the parallels in John 12:1-8, where it is Mary (the sister of Martha and Lazarus) who anoints Jesus's feet, and Luke 7:36-50 where an unnamed women, reputed to be a sinner, anoints Jesus's feet. There is also the parallel, in the Markan order and dependent on Mark's story, in Matt 26:6-13. What is notable about this story is that while Jesus receives the anointing on his head, "certain ones" (14:4 my trans.) complain about the woman's "wasting" the rare and expensive oil in order to anoint Jesus. They complain that the "pure oil of nard" (14:5 my trans.) could have been sold for more than three hundred denarii, and the money given to support the poor. Those around Jesus in this moment understand that the ointment was wasted on him, and their conclusion conflicts with Mark's view of the meaning of this anointing. This narrative of anointing is almost at the beginning of the passion narrative, and Jesus's mention in 14:8 of his burial alerts the readers one more time (after 14:1-2) that the trial and painful death of Jesus are coming in the next chapter. Not only is the death of Jesus memorialized beforehand, here the anointing by the unnamed woman is memorialized by Jesus himself: this story will be told "in memory of her" (14:9). This verse invites readers to compare Jesus's approval of the unnamed woman who anointed him with his rebukes of his male disciples elsewhere in Mark, together with their abandonment of Jesus after his arrest.

The Betrayal of Jesus by Judas (14:10-11)

More negative information about one apostle is in these two verses. Rather than the chief priests' themselves going to look for a person who would betray Jesus to them, here it is one of Jesus's apostles, whom he chose, who becomes a traitor to Jesus. He agrees to betray Jesus for a monetary reward. He will be paid in cash, with thirty silver coins. Mark does not tell his readers what happens to Judas, the traitor, after he betrays Jesus, but Matt 27:3-9 does: Judas throws down the thirty silver coins in the temple precincts, and the concern of the temple authorities is that it cannot be deposited in the temple treasury since it is "the price of blood" (Matt 27:6 my trans.), so it will be used to purchase the "potter's field" (Matt 27:10), in which indigent people can be buried. Judas's response to the promise of being paid in cash is that he now looks for the best opportunity to betray Jesus (Mark 14:11).

Preparing for the Passover (14:12-17)

Jesus, an observant Jew, wished to celebrate the Passover with his disciples, who were presumably also observant Jews. Jesus and his disciples were people from Galilee. Their observances of liturgical and other traditions of Judaism may well have been less than perfectly circumspect, as far as fellow Jews in Jerusalem were concerned,[2] but we can assume the disciples wanted to celebrate the Passover, along with Jesus. Like the episode with the colt which Jesus rode into Jerusalem (11:1b-6), the room in which Jesus and his apostles were to celebrate the Passover meal was made available to them in at least as automatic a fashion.

Jesus Predicts His Betrayal (14:18-21)

Jesus predicts his passion, death, and resurrection three times—in Mark 8, 9, and 10, and in chapter 13 Jesus predicts the destruction of the Jerusalem temple. Now Jesus reveals to his close friends and confidants that one of them will betray him. This news is painful to them. Each of them asks Jesus, "Surely it is not I?" (14:19).

The Last Supper (14:22-25)

The earliest narrative about the institution of the Eucharist or Lord's Supper is in 1 Cor 11:23-26. The next earliest is this passage. The institution of the Eucharist took place as part of a Passover meal, according to the Synoptic Gospels (though not in the Gospel of John), yet it was not actually a Passover itself.[3] The characteristic theme of the Passover meal, namely,

---

2. Vermes, *Jesus in His Jewish Context*, 42-57; as well as Freyne, *Galilee, Jesus and the Gospels*, 33-68.

3. For an extensive bibliography on the Last Supper and the Eucharist in the New Testament, see Davies and Allison, *Gospel According to Saint Matthew*, 3:478-81.

the liberation of the Hebrew people from oppression in Egypt, is not found in what we learn about the Eucharist from the New Testament.

The main presupposition of the institution of the Eucharist is Jesus's knowledge that he will depart the fellowship with his disciples shortly, even that very night. One of the principal meanings of the Eucharist, of course, is that the Eucharist continues Jesus's presence in the church after his natural human life ends. Jesus knew that he would not be with the Twelve much longer; presumably he knew he would be arrested that night. The circle of fellowship, the communion (*koinōnia*) that Jesus and his close followers have shared, would be broken. And even worse, the breaking of the fellowship of Jesus and the Twelve would be caused by one of the Twelve, namely, Judas Iscariot. The chief priests and scribes did not seek Judas out to identify him as a betrayer: Judas sought them out. Thus, here at the Last Supper there is one more instance of the disciples' not being loyal followers of Jesus. Their disloyalty ranges from the betrayal by Judas in the next passage to the threefold breaking of the promise of loyalty by Peter to the silence of the other disciples. The separation of Jesus from his disciples must have been painful for all of them (perhaps excluding Judas) but surely the most painful for Jesus. The extreme seriousness of Jesus's actions at the Last Supper is underscored by his pledge not to drink wine until he drinks it "anew in the kingdom of God" (14:25 my trans.).

Jesus Predicts Peter's Denial (14:26–31)

The liturgical celebration of the Passover concluded with the singing of a hymn, and then the disciples and Jesus went to the Mount of Olives. Following on from Jesus's prediction of Judas's betrayal in 14:18, Peter declares his loyalty to Jesus, even including his death if that were necessary (14:29, 31). Yet Jesus is just as aware of Peter's future threefold betrayal, to happen that very night, as he is of Judas's past betrayal (14:30). Incongruously, the Christian tradition has generally condemned Judas Iscariot while it has generally honored Peter. Yet in the Gospel of Mark, the risen Jesus neither encounters nor forgives Peter for his abandonment and threefold denial of association with Jesus. Despite the often-cited tradition in the Papias fragments that Mark was the interpreter and protégé of Peter,[4] the gospel attributed to Mark does not even remotely suggest to its readers that Peter would be worthy of the honor which the later church bestowed on him.

---

4. Eusebius, *Ecclesiastical History* 3.39.15.

The other disciples, however, also pledge loyalty to Jesus in a similar way (14:31b).

The Garden of Gethsemane (14:32–42)

Arguably, the most touching story in the passion narrative is the story of the pain of Christ in the garden of Gethsemane, including the contrast between the anguish of Christ's prayers and the attitude of the disciples, who are unable to stay awake. In Mark, Jesus is fully aware that he is going to be arrested, tortured, and put to a degrading death. Like anyone else, including his disciples, Jesus wishes to avoid this unjust fate at the hands of the Roman occupation authorities. This is what Jesus prays for in Mark 14:35–36. God, whom Jesus addresses as *'abba* ("Father!"), does not grant Jesus what he prays for: "that the hour might pass from him" (14:35). Jesus, however, qualified his prayer: "remove this cup from me; yet, not what I want, but what you want" (14:36). An essential part of the theology of the Gospel of Mark, as we read not only in the passion narrative but also in the three predictions of the passion, is the importance of the death of Jesus. At almost the same time as Jesus prayed that this horrible and shameful death would be taken from him, Jesus was aware that the one who was to betray him into the hands of the temple police was nearby. So according to Mark, Jesus knew all along that his betrayal, suffering, and death were coming, which is why the three predictions of the passion in chapters 8, 9, and 10 are such integral parts of Mark.

The Arrest of Jesus (14:43–52)

The arrest of Jesus took place even as Jesus was speaking to his disciples (14:43). A crowd comes, carrying swords and clubs and including the chief priests, scribes, and elders. Judas said that the one he would kiss was the one they wanted to take into custody (14:44). Thus, incongruously, this gesture of friendship and love toward Jesus becomes an act of betrayal. Jesus points out that he had been in the temple precincts every day, teaching, and yet the Jewish hierarchy did not cause him to be arrested in everyone's view, actually in the temple (14:48–49). They preferred to take Jesus by stealth, so that his arrest would not cause a riot (14:2). The disciples, now take their leave of Jesus and flee (14:50). One interesting detail is that there was a young man who was a follower of Jesus, wearing only a linen or cotton shirt; the authorities lay hands on his garment, and the young man runs away naked (14:51–52).

Jesus's Interrogation by the Sanhedrin (14:53–65)

Those who arrested Jesus bring him before the chief priest, and along with him gathered all the chief priests and elders and scribes (14:53). Peter is staying a good distance away from the proceedings against Jesus (14:54). The Sanhedrin was seeking evidence against Jesus, and they do not find any (14:54). Finally the chief priest question Jesus, asking him, "Are you the Messiah, the Son of the Blessed One?" Jesus answers, "I am, and you will see the Son of Man at the right hand of the power, coming with the clouds of heaven" (14:61–62). This affirmative answer causes the Sanhedrin to condemn him, and some of the group spit on him and hit him (14:63–65). The irony of this scene is that Jesus, claiming truthfully to be the Messiah, is rejected as a blasphemer in the highest gathering of Jewish leaders in Jerusalem. They will bring him to the Roman governor, Pontius Pilate, for a trial according to Roman law.

Peter's Denial (14:66–72)

Jesus's prophecy (14:30) that Peter would deny his association with Jesus three times (14:68, 70, 71) now comes true in this passage, and so a rooster crows (14:72). Peter realizes what he has done, as well as Jesus's prophecy of it, and he goes outside quickly and weeps. We are not told about anything else Peter does in the Gospel of Mark from this point until the end. His threefold denial of Jesus, Mark apparently thinks, has caused Peter to drop out of the story of Jesus. He will be absent from the Roman trial of Jesus, and from the crucifixion and death of Jesus; further, he will not be a party to the revelation of or the message about the resurrection of Jesus in Mark 16:1–8. It is difficult to see how this could possibly contribute to a positive assessment of Peter in the Gospel of Mark, anything that Papias would say about Mark and Peter in the second century to the contrary.

Jesus and Pontius Pilate (15:1–5)

Those who had secretly plotted against Jesus in 14:1–2 now publicly bind Jesus, take him forcibly, and hand him over to Pontius Pilate (15:1). The impromptu meeting of the Sanhedrin (14:53–65) after Jesus's arrest had not been a trial but an official interrogation by the Jerusalem authorities. They brought charges against Jesus and handed him over to Pilate to face justice under Roman law, the only law Pilate could enforce.

Pilate asks Jesus directly if he is "the king of the Jews" (15:2). Note that Pilate does not use the Hebrew or Aramaic word "Messiah." He most likely was not interested in how Jesus fit or did not fit into Jewish expectations of an anointed king, although he would have been very interested in whether Jesus was involved in setting up a Jewish kingdom, which would obviously have been in opposition to the Roman Empire. Jesus answers Pilate, "You say [that I am]" (15:2 my trans.). Pilate questions Jesus again, pointing out the many accusations brought against him, and yet Jesus makes no answer (15:5).

It was Jesus's right to make no answer, but his silence could have been interpreted by Pilate as a tacit assent to the question asked in view of the charges brought against him.

The Release of Jesus or Barabbas? (15:6–14)

Pontius Pilate would have been highly motivated to avoid creating or contributing to a Jewish riot in Jerusalem at the time of Passover. Civic unrest in Jerusalem was bad at any time, and at the time of Passover, with thousands of Jewish pilgrims in the city to observe the holiest days of the year, a civic disturbance was dangerous to all, Jews and Roman officials alike. If such a riot happened at that time, the Roman governor would have to order the soldiers to deal with the riot, which would very likely cause bloodshed. So it is quite likely that Pontius Pilate would go out of his way to avoid anything that would give any Jews an excuse to create a riot.

The custom of the Roman governor's giving up one condemned Jewish prisoner was evidently an effort to please the crowd, including the Jewish population and Jewish pilgrims to Jerusalem. The verb *apeluen* ("allow to go free") in 15:6 is in the imperfect tense, and the aspect of this verb indicates that it was an action that was not complete. Thus, the preferred translation is "he had the habit of allowing to go free," suggesting that it was a usual action of freeing a prisoner that Pilate did at the feast of Passover. The crowd preferred that Pilate free Barabbas, a convicted murderer, instead of Jesus. The crowd shouted for Jesus to be crucified. This is, to say the very least, extremely ironic. Instead of wanting to accept and glorify Jesus as a person who might lead some kind of resistance to Rome, a possibility implied by Jesus's entry into Jerusalem (Mark 11:1–10 with parallels in Matt 21:1–9; Luke 19:28–40; and John 12:12–16), now the Jerusalem crowd shouts for Jesus to suffer the most horrific death penalty from the imperial power that was oppressing them and would continue to oppress them for years to come.

It is even more striking to take careful note of the fact that Pilate never says Jesus is guilty of any crime in the Markan account. After the crowd shouts out that Jesus should be crucified, Pilate even asks the crowd, "Why? What evil thing did he do?" (15:14 my trans.). So Pilate, according to Mark, thought Jesus was innocent of any crime deserving the death penalty.

Pilate Makes a Decision (15:15), and Jesus Is Abused by Roman Soldiers (15:16–20a)

The Roman governor had asked the crowd what the penalty should be for Jesus, who, according to Mark, had not been convicted of any crime. Any crime of which Jesus was convicted in the extremely brief account of the trial in Mark 15:2–5, is not disclosed to the readers. The crowd had called more than once for Jesus's crucifixion (15:13–14). And so Pilate delivered Jesus for crucifixion, which was preceded by a horrific flogging (15:15). The purpose of the flogging, in addition to degradation, was to make it extremely painful for the condemned person to lean back on the vertical beam of the cross in an ultimately futile attempt to take some weight off the wounds in the wrists and feet in order to breathe with less difficulty.

Stripped naked for the flogging, next Jesus was led outside, dressed in a purple robe and a crown of thorns, and mocked.[5] Later the purple robe was taken away, and Jesus was dressed in his own clothing and paraded to Golgotha.

---

5. Gnilka, *Jesus of Nazareth*, 308.

The Walk to Golgotha (15:20b–21)

Evidently his flagellation had been worse than expected, as Jesus was completely exhausted. He was not able to carry the heavy horizontal beam of his cross from the Roman praetorium to Golgotha, so a visitor to Jerusalem, Simon of Cyrene, was pressed into service.

Jesus's Crucifixion (15:22–26)

The executioners now led Jesus to a place on Golgotha, which was commonly called "Place of a Skull" (15:22). He was offered wine mixed with myrrh to drink, as a sedative, which he refused (15:23). There they crucified him and divided up his garments by casting lots for them. It was "the third hour" when they crucified him, meaning nine o'clock in the morning. Over his head was an inscription: "The King of the Jews" (15:26).

Jesus on the Cross (15:27–32b)

Jesus's degradation did not stop with his flogging, with the mocking and beating from Roman soldiers, or with his being stripped of his clothing. Added to all this was the verbal abuse by people who were also crucified with Jesus, as well as by passersby and chief priests and scribes (15:29–32).

The Death of Jesus (15:33–39)

Mark notes that Jesus was crucified at nine o'clock in the morning (15:25). At noon, the "sixth hour," there was "darkness over the whole earth until the ninth hour" (15:33). At the ninth hour, namely, at 3:00 p.m., Jesus with a loud voice shouted, "My God, my God, why have you abandoned me?" (15:34 my trans.), which is a quotation from Ps 22:2. The similarity of "*Eloi*" to Elijah caused some people standing nearby to say, "He is calling for Elijah" (15:35), which also reminds readers of the connection between the pair of John the Baptizer and Jesus and the pair of Elijah and Elisha. Jesus, who had refused the wine mixed with myrrh (15:23), now drinks the sour wine (15:36). When Jesus dies, the curtain in the temple is torn in two, from top to bottom, evidently symbolizing that because of the death of Jesus, believers in him have open access to God (15:38). The Roman centurion standing facing Jesus, seeing that he had died, exclaimed, "Truly, this man was God's Son!" (15:39). Thus, Mark informs the readers that not all the people who were part of the Roman administration thought Jesus's execution was a good thing.

Women Present at the Crucifixion of Jesus (15:40–41)

The male disciples, in Matthew, Mark, and Luke, all flee the scene of Jesus's torture and death, not wanting to be associated with him. Only in the Gospel of John is a male disciple of Jesus near him when he dies. This otherwise unnamed person is called "the disciple whom Jesus loved" in John 19:26. So, the images here in Mark of the male disciples of Jesus, as they have often been in this gospel, are unfavorable. Women, however, remain faithful to Jesus as he dies on the cross. Mark 15:40–41 name three of them: "Mary Magdalene, Mary the mother of James the Less and of Joses, and Salome, who had followed him in Galilee and had ministered to him, along with many other women who had gone up with him to Jerusalem" (my trans.).

The Burial of Jesus (15:42–47)

The death of Jesus happened at or during "the ninth hour," meaning around three o'clock in the afternoon, and so Joseph of Arimathea went to Pontius Pilate to request to remove Jesus's body from the cross and to bury him in a tomb. Pilate asked the centurion to make sure Jesus had died (15:44–45), and then he gave permission to Joseph to take Jesus's body. Jesus was wrapped in a new linen cloth, and he was laid in a new tomb (15:46). Mary Magdalene and Mary the mother of Joses saw where he was buried (15:47).

Thus ended the earthly, natural life of Jesus of Nazareth, who was a teacher, preacher, healer, and gatherer of disciples. The Gospel of Mark makes clear to its readers that Jesus's conviction and death were completely unjust. The cruel Roman procedure employed to torture and kill Jesus was meant for criminals who were not Roman citizens, probably in order to make examples of them and so to discourage others from doing anything that would make life more difficult for the Roman rulers of Judea. The Roman rulers were usually willing to work with religious leaders, but they would not tolerate anything that they could interpret as sedition or disloyalty to the Roman emperor. The high concentration of Jews in Jerusalem, particularly at Passover, made it more dangerous than at other times for those who might be suspected of being disloyal to the empire.

Joachim Gnilka points out: "Two primary tendencies can be observed in the accounts of the Gospels, namely, to exonerate the Roman, Pilate, and to incriminate the Jewish side. Pilate thus acts almost against his will when he gives the order to have Jesus crucified."[6] In reality, the cause of Jesus's conviction by Pontius Pilate, Gnilka says, was "claiming the kingdom for himself."[7] Further, Gnilka writes, "Although the Gospels contain more hints than explicit statements, we may assume that it was Jesus's temple protest, his move against the money changers and the sellers of pigeons in the court of the Gentiles, that was the reason for his arrest."[8]

Thus, while certain Jewish leaders in Jerusalem may well have been afraid of the intra-Jewish ramifications of his temple protest, because of the potential of the Jewish community in Jerusalem to become disunited in the face of Roman oppression, the event of Jesus's entry into Jerusalem cannot have failed to attract attention, both Jewish and Roman, to the person and movement of Jesus. A messiah was an anointed Jewish king, and the potential for the interpretation or misinterpretation of the meaning of Jesus as a king other than the Roman emperor posed a grave threat not only to the unity of the Jewish community under Roman rule in and around Jerusalem but also to the safety of Jews there. The Jews could not afford to be in a religious war with one another. Any insurrection could have been, and later would be, put down harshly and bloodily by the Romans. So the Jewish leaders, as far as we can read in the Gospels, opted for what they believed was safest option for themselves and their community.

In contrast, it seems quite clear that Jesus did not put much stock in personal safety. Jesus was first and foremost an eschatological thinker. He looked towards the final and cataclysmic intervention of God, whenever that would happen (and he believed it to be coming soon.) The center of his teaching was the kingdom of God. During his natural life Jesus taught that God the Father, was always sovereign. The kingdom, nonetheless, was not fully present during Jesus's natural life. The full presence of the kingdom would manifest when Jesus made his second coming, when he came again as judge and savior. The second coming would be something that would take place in the future, admittedly at an unknown time. Yet Jesus preached and taught that God the Father would be fully in charge at that point in the future. Earthly governments and authorities seemed to matter

---

6. Gnilka, *Jesus of Nazareth*, 301.
7. Gnilka, *Jesus of Nazareth*, 304.
8. Gnilka, *Jesus of Nazareth*, 306.

little to Jesus. What mattered to him, and after his resurrection what mattered to his apostles and other followers, were faith in God and faithfulness to God. No matter what earthly rulers and governments would say or do, God would remain God. It was this faith and this hope that sustained Jesus during his painful and grisly suffering and death.

10

The Resurrection
Mark 16:1-8 [9-20]

This section of Mark dealing with Jesus's resurrection requires a very careful approach. Most New Testament scholars believe that Mark 16:9–20 are not an original part of the Gospel of Mark. These twelve verses are known as "the longer ending of Mark." There is also "the shorter ending of Mark," which consists of a few verses that have been assigned neither verse numbers nor a chapter number. One should take note of the fact that both the longer ending and the shorter ending of Mark include appearances to the Jesus's disciples by the risen Christ. This is very important, given that the story of the empty tomb in Mark 16:1-8 does not include an appearance of the risen Christ. It tells the readers of Mark that the tomb in which Jesus had been buried was empty, which presupposes that the resurrection happened, yet it does not tell how or exactly when it happened.

The Women at the Empty Tomb (16:1-8)

Mary Magdalene, Mary the mother of James, and Salome bought spices so that they would go to the tomb to anoint the dead body of Jesus (16:1), which they fully expected to be where Mary Magdalene had seen the body of Jesus laid to rest (15:47). They went to the tomb early on the first day of the week (Sunday), for now the Passover and the Sabbath were over. They were not doubtful about the death of Jesus, and they were clearly worried how they might be able to get into the tomb, since a large stone had been rolled in front of the tomb's entrance (16:3–4). Instead of seeing the corpse of Jesus, they saw a young man wearing a white garment. This young man told them not to be afraid. Yet his message to them was far from usual. "You are seeking Jesus of Nazareth, who was crucified. He is risen; he is not here. See the place where he was laid" (16:6 my trans.). The young man in the tomb told the women that they must tell "his disciples and Peter that he is going ahead of you into Galilee. There you will see him, just as I told you" (16:7 my trans.). And, very notably, instead of doing just as the young man told them in the tomb, the women flee from the tomb, "for they had trembling and amazement. And they said nothing to anyone, for they were afraid" (16:8 my trans.).

This last sentence, concerning the trembling, amazement, and especially the silence of the women who were at the tomb of Jesus, raises many questions, especially when we consider the parallel empty tomb stories in Matt 28:1–8 and Luke 24:1–12. In Matt 28:8 the women exit the tomb "with fear and great joy," and in Luke 24:9 the women "leaving the tomb, told all these things to the Eleven and to all the others" (my trans.). In Mark 16:8, it is not said that the women who went to the empty tomb ever told the male disciples anything. If the original ending of Mark is at the end of 16:8, then the lack of transmission of any information about the empty tomb or the resurrection of Jesus to the male disciples is—to say the very least—very striking.

In comparison with other narratives of the empty tomb as well as with several resurrection appearances of Jesus, the importance of the women's failure to convey the fact of resurrection to the male disciples cannot be overstated. The apostles are the ones who would be sent out in mission. It is the risen Christ and the message about the death and resurrection of Christ that caused the disciples of Jesus to be sent out (*apostellein*) as apostles (*apostoloi*). Without that miraculous, supernatural message, there is nothing that the apostles would be sent out to do. The tasks that apostles were supposed to do were to proclaim, teach, and otherwise spread "the good news of Jesus Christ," which was the exact original title of the Gospel of Mark (1:1).

Other Endings of Mark

Mark 16:9–20 is called the longer ending of Mark. It is included in the 28th Nestle-Aland edition of the Greek New Testament, which is the standard critical text that most New Testament scholars use, but these twelve verses are printed between double square brackets. This edition, in its explanation of signs and abbreviations, says the following: "The text enclosed in double square brackets cannot be considered authentic."[1] The reason for this judgment is that, while these twelve verses are in a majority of the manuscripts of Mark, they do not appear in the earliest manuscripts. Those who evaluate the transmission of the text on the basis of ancient manuscripts and other witnesses to the text (such as early translations into other languages and quotations from early Christian writers) generally reject Mark 16:9–20 as inauthentic because text critics prefer the readings of even a small number of the earliest manuscripts over the readings of a larger number of later witnesses to the text. As a result, several modern translations of the New Testament include 16:9–20 not in the regular text of Mark but in a bracketed part of the text, or in a footnote.

The "shorter ending of Mark" clearly does not appear to be an authentic ending. It says, in part, that Jesus sent out "those around Peter" and that they made "from east to west, the sacred and imperishable proclamation of eternal salvation."

There is another ending of Mark that appears in a manuscript of Mark in the Freer Gallery of Art in the Smithsonian Institution in Washington, DC. This ending is known as the "Freer Logion." It also portrays the risen Jesus speaking to his disciples, and quite jarringly he says, "The term of years of Satan's power has been fulfilled, but other terrible things draw near," and he further speaks of "the spiritual and imperishable glory of righteousness that is in heaven." The Freer Logion appears to convey neither authentic material from Jesus nor the actual, original ending of the Gospel of Mark.

The one thing that these three inauthentic endings of Mark have in common is that the risen Jesus appears to several of the male disciples and speaks. In the longer ending of Mark, there is the ascension of Jesus into heaven (16:9–20), which has affinities with Luke 24:50–53 and Acts 1:6–11. So it is clear that those who created these inauthentic endings of Mark were dissatisfied with the ending at 16:8: "they said nothing to anyone, for they were afraid."

---

1. Nestle-Aland, *Novum Testamentum Graece*, 28th rev. ed., 880.

The Resurrection

Thus, the most important question is not whether Mark 16:9–20, the shorter ending, or the Freer Logion are authentic endings of Mark, but whether or not the original Gospel of Mark really ended with 16:1–8. That is a harder question to answer, and one may ask whether we in the twenty-first century actually have enough textual or other historical information to answer that question, or with what level of probability we could answer it.

Nonetheless, my opinion is that the original ending of this gospel was Mark 16:1–8. It is an unusual ending, to be sure. The uniqueness of the ending at 16:8 is an excellent explanation of the reasons that Mark 16:9–20, the shorter ending of Mark, and the Freer Logion were created. The resurrection of Jesus was clearly a presupposition of the empty tomb story in 16:1–8. But Mark's silence concerning any rehabilitation of the male disciples after their fleeing upon Jesus's arrest and given Peter's threefold denial is jarring. Even more jarring is Mark's silence about the male disciples' seeing the empty tomb or having any firsthand or secondhand knowledge of Jesus's resurrection. Still more jarring is the fact that the apostles (*apostoloi*) were not sent out (*apostellein*) in Mark by the risen Jesus to proclaim his resurrection to other people in the world. This strongly suggests that there was little or no linking in Mark between the apostles and either the resurrected Jesus or the event of the resurrection itself.

Nonetheless, the way the Gospel of Mark deals with the apostles should not obscure what is important in the way that Jesus is portrayed. Jesus died an unjust death. Despite the fact that Jesus's disciples hardly understood him and were unfaithful to him during his suffering and death, none of that takes away from the importance of his life, his deeds of power, his teaching, and the resurrection itself.

11

Reflections on Mark as a Whole

AT THE END OF this chapter of this guide to Mark, our journey together through the Gospel according to Mark is finished. My journey with this gospel is continuing. I hope that your journey through this book does not mean that you are done with the Gospel of Mark. I hope that you will continue to read Mark and the other Gospels and that you will continue to gather insights about the Gospel of Mark and about Jesus. Before I lay this portion of my work on Mark aside to go on to my next project (which may be a medium-sized commentary on Mark), I want to note carefully what I have found to be memorable and important as I read and interpret Mark.

The writer of Mark had an unshakable belief that Jesus was the Son of God and that by his works of proclaiming the gospel and healing the sick (and doing other deeds of power), he was actively pursuing God the Father's agenda of bringing about an awareness of the coming kingdom of God. Indeed, with Jesus's presence and work, the kingdom was actually, if partially, present. The kingdom of God was, as the writer of Mark thought, both present in the person of Jesus and also not yet fully realized. The words of Rudolf Bultmann are memorable: "But what are the signs of the time? He himself! *His presence, his deeds, his message!*"[1] The message of Jesus, of which we can read a great deal in the Gospel of Mark, is a message about the presence of God, a presence which broke into the lived experience of those whom Jesus encountered, both in word and deed. The two great parts

---

1. Bultmann, *Theology of the New Testament*, 1:7. The italics are in the English translation.

of Jesus's ministry, during his earthly life as Mark presents it, were proclaiming the good news of God and doing deeds of power. The importance of both parts of Jesus's life and work cannot be denied.

Yet there was also a third part of what Jesus did. He recruited and called people whom Mark often refers to as "the Twelve" or the apostles. The Gospel of Matthew clearly seems to prefer the term "disciples" (and, of course, "disciples" [*discipuli*] means "students"), because that author wants to emphasize the fact that the twelve apostles were taught by Jesus, and after Jesus's death, it is eleven of them who will become the honored, official interpreters of Jesus and his message. The high level of honor and authority that the Gospel of Matthew was quite willing to bestow on the eleven apostles was a level of honor and authority that the writer of Mark declined to confer on anybody in the early church. Thus, one of the points of greatest importance to note about Mark is that Mark has a point of view about "the Twelve" or the apostles. It is generally a negative point of view.

As mentioned earlier in this book, the anonymous writer of Mark has an unshakable point of view that identified Elijah and Elisha as the biblical models that John the Baptizer and Jesus imitated. We do not now have any way of knowing whether or not John the Baptizer or Jesus actually took Elijah and Elisha as their models, but we can say that the writer of Mark was deeply convinced that Jesus was like Elisha, who was a greater miracle worker than Elijah. And in Mark and the other New Testament Gospels, John the Baptizer was very much in the prophetic tradition of preaching the justice and impending judgment of God and, consequently, the need for Israel to repent. So there appears to be a good fit between the pairs Elijah and Elisha and John the Baptizer and Jesus.[2]

What Did Jesus Do?

There are innumerable ways to study the Gospel of Mark as a whole. I will now present my view about Mark. At this point, let me take a look backwards in Mark, to be as clear as possible about what Jesus did in his natural, human lifetime.

---

2. Of course, it is easier to affirm that there is a fit than it is to determine whether the writer of Mark discovered the fit or constructed the fit.

Jesus Proclaimed the Kingdom of God

Many of Jesus's parables, particularly in chapter 4 of Mark, are about the kingdom of God. Several of these parables are about the astonishing growth of the kingdom of God, such as the parable of the mustard seed or the parable of the seed growing secretly. Very notably, in Jesus's theology, according to Mark, the kingdom is partly here (or "inaugurated") because of the coming and presence of Jesus. Probably miracles are evidence of the presence of the kingdom. The full presence of the kingdom will be in the second coming of Christ.

Jesus Did Deeds of Power

As the late Wolfgang Roth pointed out, Elijah did eight deeds of power, and Elisha did sixteen deeds of power. When Jesus does sixteen deeds of power, the people say, "He has done all things well" (Mark 7:37). Then Jesus does eight more deeds of power, ending with the resurrection in Mark 16:1–8. Jesus is therefore a prolific worker of deeds of power, and so he appears to be in the tradition of Elisha, but actually greater than both Elijah and Elisha. When quite a few people saw the miracles that Jesus did, they had faith in him as Son of God, namely, as the anointed king or Messiah, who would be a successor to King David. The miracle stories in Mark connect Jesus in two important ways with traditions in the Greco-Roman world. First of all, Jesus does miracles because he is identified as a successor of Elisha, the prophet of Israel who did the most miracles. Jesus is not just a miracle worker: he is a *Jewish* miracle worker. His miracles show connection after connection with Elijah and miracles in the Hebrew Bible. Jews and other readers of the Hebrew Bible, in Hebrew or in Greek, could be expected to see the connections between Jesus and miracle workers of the Hebrew Bible. The connection of Jesus with John the Baptizer, together with Elisha's connection to Elijah, make it unmistakable to Jewish or proselyte readers or hearers of Mark that Jesus is connected in extremely important ways to what would come to be called the Old Testament. God was renewing Israel in a new way by sending Jesus as a miracle worker in the tradition of Elisha, who clearly stood in the tradition of Elijah.

Secondly, the miracle stories in Mark portray Jesus again and again as having divine power to heal as well as to perform other miracles. This power, demonstrated to the readers of Mark in miracle stories, makes clear to those in the Greco-Roman world—both inside and outside Judaism—that Jesus had powers given him by God—however God was understood—that set Jesus apart from other human beings. Non-Jews reading Mark could comprehend the power that Jesus had, whether or not they knew anything or cared anything about the God of Israel. Some of the people Jesus healed were not Jews but were part of the wider religious scene in the Greco-Roman world. The miracle stories could be understood in various ways by Jews, because of the strong connection with Elijah and Elisha. And the miracle stories could be understood as manifestations of divine power by Gentiles, quite apart from the heritage and traditions of Judaism. So Mark's extremely prominent inclusion of miracle stories—miracles of healing, miracles of provision, and nature miracles, as well as the resurrection of Jesus himself—had the strong potential of appealing to more than one audience. It is difficult to imagine that appealing to a wide audience was not an intentional part of the composition and the rhetorical purpose of the Gospel of Mark.

Jesus Chose "the Twelve"

It is clear that Jesus chose "the Twelve," also known as the apostles or the disciples. In the calling of the first apostles, namely, Simon, Andrew, James, and John, Mark does not say or even suggest that Jesus used what is now called "due diligence" in choosing his closest followers. Jesus seems to have done the opposite of that. Perhaps because of Jesus's lack of care in choosing the Twelve, the Twelve have major trouble understanding Jesus's own conception of his messianic identity. Indeed Peter, who becomes the chief of the apostles, first has trouble agreeing with Jesus about Jesus's own mission; later, Peter denies Jesus three times. Finally, Peter and the others abandon Jesus when it gets dangerous, after his arrest. It would be impossible to dissociate Mark's treatment of the apostles from the overall rhetoric of Mark.

Many people nowadays do share a perspective with Mark. In the wake of many negative things that are said about churches and leaders of churches and denominations of all sorts, partly because of numerous scandals, the critique that Mark has for "the Twelve" or "the apostles" is compelling. We all recognize that churches have good moments and bad moments. Mark chose to make its readers aware of the apostles' bad moments.

Jesus Predicted His Own Suffering and Death

The three predictions of the passion in Mark can be cited as follows: 8:27–33; 9:30–37; and 10:32–34. Note that in the second and third predictions of the passion, the apostles do not take issue with the suffering that Jesus says he is going to undergo, but they are silent about it. In the first passion prediction, Peter actually rebukes Jesus (8:33). None of the apostles can have been happy with Jesus's prediction of his own suffering and death, which is made all the more certain by his going to Jerusalem with his followers at the time of Passover. Yet the tradition of Jesus's voluntarily going to his death and, thus, offering himself as a self-sacrifice seems to be a firm part of both the synoptic tradition and the tradition in the Gospel of John. Jesus's death as a self-sacrifice does not appear to have been something that the final editors or compilers of any of the Gospels made up out of whole cloth. It appears to me to be authentic Jesus-tradition.

Jesus Predicted His Resurrection from Death

The three passion predictions by Jesus include the predictions of his resurrection in 8:31, 9:31, and 10:34. The resurrection of Jesus in 16:1–8 is the final "deed of power" in the Gospel of Mark. There is no reason to believe that Jesus's prediction of his own resurrection from death is not an authentic part of the tradition of sayings of Jesus. Of course, the resurrection of Jesus is an important part of early Christian tradition, more generally. First of all there is 1 Cor 15:3–8, which includes an eyewitness account by Paul, who claims—quite independently of all other writers—to have seen the risen Christ. Also fully independent of the Gospels are passages about the resurrection of Christ in 1 Pet 1:3–6 and Rev 1:4–5.

Jesus Predicted His Second Coming

The second coming of Jesus is well known to us from 1 Thess 4:13—5:3; 2 Thess 1:7–10; 2:8; Titus 2:11–13; and Rev 1:7–8. In Mark it is found in the Little Apocalypse or Markan Apocalypse in 13:1–37. Mark 13:4–27 is an "apocalyptic timetable." It describes cosmic events that will take place before and during the second coming of Christ. The synoptic parallels to Mark 13 are Matt 24 and Luke 21. Matthew's and Luke's accounts are based on Mark.

Reflections on Mark as a Whole

What Seems to Be Behind Mark's Criticism of the Apostles?

I have laid emphasis on Mark's criticism of the apostles at several places in this book. This criticism cannot possibly be an unimportant part of Mark. We readers of Mark may not like it, but we certainly cannot ignore it. First of all, the strong criticism of the apostles was a strong critique of the church that the writer of Mark knew in the first century CE. The most serious criticism that could possibly be made of the apostles, who were taught directly by Jesus, is that they doubted the resurrection of Jesus when it was first taught them. In the other Gospels, the apostles refuse to believe in the resurrection of Jesus until they see the risen Christ themselves—including all the apostles, not just Thomas in John 20:24–28. Here in Mark there is an even more serious criticism of the apostles: they were not informed of the resurrection by the women at the empty tomb! Still worse, after they flee after Jesus's arrest in the passion narrative, and after Peter's denial of his association with Jesus, the apostles do not reappear in the Gospel of Mark. What does this imply about their faithfulness to the message that they later proclaimed to the world? It was, moreover, not only the male apostles who were silent about the resurrection; even the faithful women, who actually went to the empty tomb, "said nothing to anybody, for they were afraid" (16:8).

Other Aspects of Mark's Theology

The leading aspect of the theology of the Gospel of Mark is Christology, namely, the understanding of the person of Jesus.[3] Without a birth or infancy story in Mark, Jesus seems to burst onto the scene in Galilee: the prehistory of Jesus consists only of prophecies from the books of Malachi and Isaiah, which point the writer of Mark to John the Baptizer, the forerunner of Jesus. Then, just as the powerful Elijah gave way to Elisha, who was even more powerful, the powerful John the Baptizer gives way in the narrative of Mark to the far more powerful Jesus. John did not perform miracles to show his power; he preached against sin and sinners! Jesus preached too,

---

3. For a full description and analysis of the theology of Mark, see especially Telford, *Theology*, 30–163; and Garland, *Theology of Mark's Gospel*; along with shorter analyses in Black, *Mark's Gospel*, 177–88; Matera, *Theology*, 5–25; Grant, *Earliest Gospel*, 148–74; Taylor, *Gospel According to St. Mark*, 114–29; Schulz, "Mark's Significance"; and Strecker, *Theology*, 343–64.

but the more famous aspect of his ministry was his many deeds of power. These deeds of power show Mark's readers again and again the power of Jesus. Jesus's ministry was inaugurated at his baptism, at which God the Father addressed Jesus in the second person singular: "You are my Son, the beloved; in you I am well pleased" (1:11 my trans.). So then the high status of Jesus was that he was Son of God, and as such, beloved by God. The many deeds of power, first the sixteen (like Elisha's) and then eight more (like Elijah and Elisha's miracles added together) demonstrate Jesus's status as the unique Son of God. An important part of Jesus's status was the fact that he had an earthly and natural life, which was ended by Roman execution. Yet the greatest miracle of all was Jesus's resurrection, in which Jesus, having died, became immortal. So the uniqueness of Jesus as Son of God is, I believe, the theme in Mark that outranks all the others. It is the reason for all the miracle stories.

I have said a great deal about the fallibility of Jesus's disciples in Mark. The disciples and other followers of Jesus, such as they are in Mark, are as close as Mark gets to an image of the church. Much has been said about how Pauline the Gospel of Mark is,[4] but, to the contrary, I do not think that the writer of Mark would agree with Paul's famous analogy that the church is "the body of Christ" (1 Cor 12). Further, I am not convinced that the writer of Mark would agree with Paul (and with the Gospel of John) that the risen Christ has bestowed the Holy Spirit on the church. So, if it were true that the Gospel of Mark was strongly influenced by Paul, one would expect that Mark would agree with Paul on those two important theological points.

Closely intertwined with Jesus's parables about the kingdom of God is the perception that the kingdom of God was not fully present during the natural lifetime of Jesus. The seeds of the kingdom were being planted by Jesus himself as well as his disciples, but the kingdom was not there yet. According to Mark, Jesus believed and his parables teach that God's kingdom was a kingdom that was coming and partially present—certainly prone to vigorous growth, yet not fully present.

The way the Gospel of Mark seems to function is that while it looks like a biography of Jesus, it is more. It is a persuasive book that invites its readers to become followers of Jesus, or better followers of Jesus. It tells of the roots of Jesus's mission in the Hebrew Bible (Old Testament), especially in the extended *imitatio* of Elijah and Elisha by John the Baptizer and Jesus.

---

4. I refer my readers to Wischmeyer et al., *Paul and Mark* and to Becker et al., *Mark and Paul*. The majority of these essays are in English, and the rest are in German.

And it shows that Jesus, as a worker of deeds of power, did the same number of miracles as Elijah's and Elisha's added together. Even more important is that Jesus's deeds of power were greater than those of the miracle-working prophets, for Jesus's powerful deeds culminated in the greatest miracle of all: his resurrection from death to eternal life. Yet even as stupendous as the resurrection of Jesus was, as Mark points out, the first reaction from the women at the empty tomb to news of the resurrection was fear, amazement, and lack of belief, resulting in their silence. The Gospel of Mark ends with the women at the tomb of Jesus not saying anything to anybody about his resurrection, and the male apostles not having even heard about it.

The ending of Mark, if it was at 16:8 (as I believe it was), is part of its rhetorical power. This ending of Mark invites the readers of this gospel to see in some detail the mistake that the women at the tomb made—because of their fear—and invites the readers, who have been enabled to know that the resurrection really did take place, along with Jesus's death, to become better and better followers of Jesus, by being stronger and stronger believers in the crucified and resurrected Jesus. As some of us know either from growing up in the church or from taking part in church life as adults—as well as from many other settings—we can learn to follow Jesus better from both positive and negative examples of discipleship. The Gospel of Mark provides one great, shining, positive example, and quite a few negative examples. The power of the Gospel of Mark, including its extremely open-ended conclusion, is that it continues to invite us to become better and better followers of Jesus, despite the fact that dealing with some other followers of Jesus has been and surely continues to be a challenge.

Current Ways to Understand Mark's Theology

There are many ways of understanding the thought of the author, compiler, or editor of Mark, perhaps as many as there are scholars who write on the Gospel of Mark. Among these presentations of Mark's theology, there are two recent ones that stand out among the rest.

William R. Telford has spent many years of his life teaching and writing on Mark at the University of Newcastle, in England. His monograph *The Theology of the Gospel of Mark* (1999) devotes 134 pages to a chapter called "The Theology of Mark."[5] Telford analyzes and responds to the many avenues of Markan scholarship since the beginning of the twentieth

---

5. Telford, *Theology of the Gospel*, 30–163.

century, when truly modern scholarship on Mark began with William Wrede's highly debated and very influential book from 1901 on the messianic secret.[6] Wrede showed that the messianic secrecy motif, in which Jesus orders his disciples and the persons he heals not to tell anybody about the healings he has performed, came fundamentally not from Jesus of Nazareth but from the writer of Mark. Wrede thus showed over a century ago that Mark could no longer be considered a simple, straightforward book: Mark had an identifiable authorial intent and point of view.

Telford's theological analysis of Mark focuses on its historical setting, its Christology, the original message of Jesus, and finally the purpose of the Gospel of Mark. According to Telford, as well as others, there were multiple Christologies among early churches, which is not hard to believe since people came to believe in Jesus from a variety of backgrounds, both Gentile and Jewish. In contrast with Wolfgang Roth, William Telford believes that

> the author of Mark's Gospel writes as a representative of a Pauline-influenced Gentile Christianity which viewed Jesus (and, by means of the secrecy motif, invites the reader to view him) as the divine "Son of God" who came to suffer and die on the cross. This Christology is in tension both with Jewish estimates of Jesus (teacher, prophet and healer) as well as Jewish-Christian ones.

Thus, the writer of Mark, Telford argues, rejected the political overtones of Jesus as a "Son of David" (meaning a king in the line of David) in favor of understanding Jesus as "Son of God." Thus Mark's Christology, as Telford sees it, is more universalistic and less nationalistic. Jesus is a or the Son of God, and so is a figure who would bring salvation to all who accept him as such.

The large monograph by David E. Garland, *A Theology of Mark's Gospel: Good News about Jesus the Messiah, the Son of God* (2015), which runs to 651 pages, including 52 pages of bibliography, not only analyzes the usual theological themes in the Gospel of Mark; it is also an extended introduction and "A Literary and Theological Reading of Mark's Gospel,"[7] including a commentary on passage after passage in Mark, dealing with the myriad historical, literary, and especially theological issues in that gospel. Closely attuned to the theological reading of Mark is the introduction, including material on Mark's authorship and historical setting. Toward the end of the book, Garland offers a full treatment of Mark 16:1–8, including of the

---

6. Wrede, *Messianic Secret*.
7. Garland, *Theology of Mark's Gospel*, 99–178.

crucial issue of whether 16:8 was the original ending of Mark. Garland's admirable monograph deals with the theological issues in Mark, including the Christology of Mark, the meaning of the kingdom of God in Mark, the messianic secret, eschatology, the meaning of discipleship, and what the mission of Jesus was, according to Mark. Garland deals with Mark with equal facility as he analyzes the early Christian statements about the Gospel of Mark, the question of the dating of Mark, the original location from which or for which Mark was written, and other questions both historical and literary.

What one can discern that is in common between Telford's and Garland's carefully written books, along with the writings of quite a few other New Testament scholars, is this: Standing behind the written Gospel According to Mark that we have are a variety of traditions, many if not most of which were rooted in oral traditions passed on in churches. Arguably, some of these Jesus-sayings and accounts of episodes in Jesus's life had their roots in what was remembered and taught by Peter and other apostles in the first century. The writer of Mark made selections from many of these oral and possibly written traditions. To these oral and written traditions that went decades back, perhaps into the life of the historical Jesus, Mark did not hesitate to add new traditions, such as the frequent commands by Jesus to be silent about his miracles during his natural lifetime. To put it as simply as possible, the author of Mark could make substantial use of old traditions about what Jesus said and did, and the very same author could also write and include new material. All of this material, both old and new, is part of the unique collage of the Gospel of Mark. Going back to Karl Ludwig Schmidt, it is clear that individual units are discernible to most New Testament scholars. And yet, as these interesting individual pieces of Mark are read together in the order in which we have them, the pieces certainly can be seen to make up the whole of Mark. A good example of this is Christology. It certainly has been shown that there are several christological ideas standing behind the text of Mark, some of them being christological ideas to which the writer of Mark was opposed. Nonetheless as the pieces of Mark are read together in the order and within the context of Mark as a whole, we can say that Mark as a whole has a Christology of its own.

Conclusion

Finally, Mark has an overall message that is, to my thinking, unique. It presents Jesus as a worthy and far greater successor to Elijah, Elisha, and John the Baptizer. Jesus's deeds of power, as presented in Mark, cannot possibly be unrelated to the deeds of power by Elijah and Elisha. Yet, in contrast to Elijah and Elisha, and also to John the Baptizer, Jesus's presence and work are not specifically for the renewal of the nation of Israel or for the renewal of Jewish life. Jesus's life and ministry had as its context living as a Jew within the early Roman Empire. He went to his death apparently voluntarily, since he went to Jerusalem at the time of Passover, with the Romans in charge in Jerusalem. The things Jesus did in Jerusalem, particularly in his "triumphal entry" and in what has been called the "cleansing of the temple"—not forgetting his debates with Pharisees, scribes, and Sadducees—were extremely provocative. I do not believe that Jesus was ignorant of how dangerous it was for him in Jerusalem, with thousands of Jewish pilgrims in the city, and with the Roman governor making serious efforts to "keep a lid on things" in the city at the time of Passover, in order to avoid a bloody Jewish revolt against the Roman occupation government. At the same time in which Mark tells us much about Jesus's encounters in Jerusalem, ending in his arrest, trial, and death, Mark also tells us of Jesus's own predictions of his suffering, death, and resurrection. So Mark seems to be fully in harmony with the other three New Testament Gospels when he deals with Jesus's death as a voluntary self-offering.

Perhaps most striking of all is the way Mark presents the disciples of Jesus, both female and male, who found it deeply painful that Jesus went to his unjust death, then found it either incomprehensible or unbelievable that Jesus would have been resurrected after his death and burial. Does the writer of Mark give the readers any indication that either the women who went to Jesus's tomb or the apostles, who did not go to the tomb, would somehow become leaders in the church after Jesus's resurrection? I do not see any indication of this in the text of Mark. And yet, if Mark was written around the year 70 of our era, then the author of Mark clearly knew of the existence of the apostolic church, which came into being shortly after Jesus's resurrection. The church had been in existence for about four decades when Mark was written. So the church cannot have been unknown to Mark. Thus, Mark's handling of the repeated foibles of the apostles does not appear to be an accident but quite intentional.

Reflections on Mark as a Whole

So, as the Gospel According to Mark concludes in its unique and open-ended way, Mark suggests that since they have read about the life and work of Jesus, ending with his arrest, trial, death, and resurrection, the readers are now insiders to what went on in the circle of Jesus's friends and enemies during his life and death and also shortly after his resurrection. And so the readers of Mark, even readers in our century, are invited to become followers—or better followers—of Jesus, and to carry on his work of bringing peace, reconciliation, and healing to the world in which we live now. The narrative of Jesus and his ministry is important because this narrative gives the readers of Mark example after example of Jesus's compassion toward his fellow human beings. That much of the time the apostles do not do a good job of following Jesus's example may suggest to us as we read Mark that we might very well do better at following Jesus in our time than they did in theirs.

Bibliography

Achtemeier, Paul J. *Invitation to Mark: A Commentary on the Gospel of Mark with Complete Text from "The Jerusalem Bible."* Image Books. Garden City, NY: Doubleday, 1978.
———. *Mark.* 2nd rev. enl. ed. Proclamation Commentaries. Philadelphia: Fortress, 1986.
———. "The Origin and Function of the Pre-Markan Miracle Catenae." *Journal of Biblical Literature* 91 (1972) 198–221.
———. "Toward the Isolation of Pre-Markan Miracle Catenae." *Journal of Biblical Literature* 89 (1970) 265–91.
Aland, Barbara, and Kurt Aland, eds. *Novum Testamentum Graece.* 27th rev. ed. Stuttgart: Deutsche Bibelgesellschaft, 1993.
———, eds. *Novum Testamentum Graece.* 28th rev. ed. Stuttgart: Deutsche Bibelgesellschaft, 2012.
Aland, Barbara, et al., eds. *The Greek New Testament.* 5th rev. ed. Stuttgart: Deutsche Bibelgesellschaft, 2014.
Aland, Kurt, ed. *Synopsis of the Four Gospels: English Edition.* New York: American Bible Society, 1982; revised printing, 1985.
———, ed. *Synopsis Quattuor Evangeliorum.* 15th ed. Stuttgart: Deutsche Bibelgesellschaft, 1996.
Augustine of Hippo, St. *The Harmony of the Gospels.* In vol. 6 of *The Nicene and Post-Nicene Fathers*, 1st ser., edited by Philip Schaff, 6:65–236. 14 vols. 1886–1889. Reprint, Grand Rapids: Eerdmans, 1979.
Beavis, Mary Ann. *Mark.* Paideia Commentaries on the New Testament. Grand Rapids: Baker Academic, 2011.
———. *Mark's Audience: The Literary and Social Setting of Mark 4.11–12.* Journal for the Study of the New Testament Supplement Series 33. Sheffield, UK: JSOT Press, 1989.
Becker, Eve-Marie, et al., eds. *Mark and Paul: Comparative Essays Part II; For and Against Pauline Influence on Mark.* Beihefte zur Zeitschrift für die neutestamentliche Wissenschaft 199. Berlin: de Gruyter, 2014.
Bernier, Jonathan. *Rethinking the Dates of the New Testament: The Evidence for Early Composition.* Grand Rapids: Baker Academic, 2022.
Best, Ernest. *Following Jesus: Discipleship in the Gospel of Mark.* Journal for the Study of the New Testament Supplement Series 4. Sheffield: JSOT Press, 1981.
Black, C. Clifton. *Mark.* Abingdon New Testament Commentaries. Nashville: Abingdon, 2011.
———. *Mark's Gospel: History, Theology, Interpretation.* Grand Rapids: Eerdmans, 2023.

Bock, Darrell. *Mark*. New Cambridge Bible Commentary. Cambridge: Cambridge University Press, 2015.
Borg, Marcus J. *Conflict, Holiness, and Politics in the Teachings of Jesus*. Harrisburg, PA: Trinity, 1998.
———. *Jesus: Uncovering the Life, Teachings, and Relevance of a Religious Revolutionary*. San Francisco: HarperOne, 2006.
Boring, M. Eugene. *Mark: A Commentary*. The New Testament Library. Louisville: Westminster John Knox, 2006.
Bornkamm, Günther. *Jesus of Nazareth*. Translated by I. and F. McLuskey with J. M. Robinson. London: Hodder & Stoughton, 1960.
Branscomb, B. Harvie. *The Gospel of Mark*. Moffatt New Testament Commentary. London: Hodder & Stoughton,1937.
Bryan, Christopher. *A Preface to Mark: Notes on the Gospel in Its Literary and Cultural Settings*. New York: Oxford University Press, 1993.
Bultmann, Rudolf. *The History of the Synoptic Tradition*. Translated by John Marsh. New York: Harper & Row, 1963.
———. *The Theology of the New Testament*. Translated by Kendrick Grobel. 2 vols. New York: Scribner, 1951–1955.
Burkill, T. A. *New Light on the Earliest Gospel: Seven Markan Studies*. Cornell University Press, 1972.
Burridge, Richard A. *What Are the Gospels? A Comparison with Graeco-Roman Biography*. 3rd ed. 20th anniversary ed. Waco, TX: Baylor University Press, 2020.
Byrne, Brendan, SJ. *A Costly Freedom: A Theological Reading of Mark's Gospel*. Collegeville, MN: Liturgical, 2008.
Carroll, John T. *Jesus and the Gospels: An Introduction*. Louisville: Westminster John Knox, 2016.
Carter, Warren. *Mark*. Wisdom Commentary 42. Collegeville, MN: Liturgical, 2019.
Chilton, Bruce. *Rabbi Jesus: An Intimate Biography*. New York: Doubleday, 2000.
Chilton, Bruce, et al., eds. *A Comparative Handbook to the Gospel of Mark*. The New Testament Gospels in Their Judaic Contexts 1. Leiden: Brill, 2010.
Cole, R. Alan. *Mark: An Introduction and Commentary*. 2nd ed. Tyndale New Testament Commentaries 2. Downers Grove, IL: IVP Academic, 2007.
Collins, Adela Yarbro. *The Beginning of the Gospel: Probings of Mark in Context*. 1992. Reprint, Eugene, OR: Wipf & Stock, 2001.
———. *Mark: A Commentary*. Hermeneia. Minneapolis: Fortress, 2007.
Collins, Adela Yarbro, and John J. Collins. *King and Messiah as Son of God: Divine, Human, and Angelic Messianic Figures in Biblical and Related Literature*. Grand Rapids: Eerdmans, 2008.
Collins, Raymond F. *Introduction to the New Testament*. Garden City, NY: Doubleday, 1983.
Cranfield, C. E. B. *The Gospel According to Saint Mark*. Cambridge Greek Testament Commentary. 1959. 4th impression with revised additional supplementary notes. Cambridge: Cambridge University Press, 1972.
Crawford, Barry S., and Merrill P. Miller, eds. *Redescribing the Gospel of Mark*. Early Christianity and Its Literature 22. Atlanta: SBL Press, 2017.
Culpepper, R. Alan. *Mark*. Smith & Helwys Bible Commentary. Macon, GA: Smith & Helwys, 2007.

BIBLIOGRAPHY

Davies, W. D., and Dale C. Allsion. *A Critical and Exegetical Commentary on the Gospel According to Saint Matthew*. 3 vols. International Critical Commentary. Edinburgh: T. & T. Clark, 1988–1997.

Dewey, Joanna. *Markan Public Debate: Literary Technique, Concentric Structure, and Theology in Mark 2:1—3:6*. Society of Biblical Literature Dissertation Series 48. Chico, CA: Scholars, 1980.

Dibelius, Martin. *From Tradition to Gospel*. Translated in collaboration with the author by Bertram Lee Woolf. 1934. Reprint, Library of Theological Translations. Cambridge: James Clarke, 2022.

Donahue, John R., SJ, and Daniel J. Harrington, SJ. *The Gospel of Mark*. Sacra Pagina, 2. Collegeville, MN: Liturgical, 2002.

Donfried, Karl Paul. *Who Owns the Bible? Toward the Recovery of a Christian Hermeneutic*. Companions to the New Testament. New York: Crossroad, 2006.

Driggers, Ira Brent. *Following God through Mark: Theological Tension in the Second Gospel*. Louisville: Westminster John Knox, 2007.

Dunn, James D. G. *Jesus, Paul, and the Law: Studies in Mark and Galatians*. Louisville: Westminster John Knox, 1990.

———. *A New Perspective on Jesus: What the Quest for the Historical Jesus Missed*. Acadia Studies in Bible and Theology. Grand Rapids: Baker Academic, 2005.

Dykstra, Tom. *Mark, Canonizer of Paul: A New Look at Intertextuality in Mark's Gospel*. St. Paul, MN: OCABS, 2012.

Easton, Burton Scott. *The Gospel Before the Gospels*. Bishop Paddock Lectures. New York: Scribner, 1928.

Edwards, James R. *The Gospel According to Mark*. Pillar New Testament Commentaries. Grand Rapids: Eerdmans, 2002.

Eichrodt, Walther. *Theology of the Old Testament*. 2 vols. Translated by J. A. Baker. Old Testament Library. Philadelphia: Westminster, 1961–1967.

Elliott, J. K. *The Language and Style of the Gospel of Mark: An Edition of C. H. Turner's "Notes on Marcan Usage" Together with Other Comparable Studies*. Supplements to Novum Testamentum 71. Leiden: Brill, 1993.

Evans, Craig A. *Mark 8:27—16:20*. Word Biblical Commentary 34B. Nashville: Nelson, 2001.

Fischer, Bonifatius, et al., eds. *Biblia sacra: iuxta Vulgatam versionem*. 4th ed. Stuttgart: Deutsche Bibelgesellschaft, 1994.

Focant, Camille. *The Gospel According to Mark: A Commentary*. Translated by Leslie Robert Keylock. Eugene, OR: Pickwick Publications, 2012.

Francis, Pope. *The Gospel of Mark: A Spiritual and Pastoral Reading*. Maryknoll, NY: Orbis, 2020.

Freyne, Sean. *Galilee, Jesus and the Gospels: Literary Approaches and Historical Investigations*. Philadelphia: Fortress, 1988.

García Martínez, Florentino, ed. *The Dead Sea Scrolls Translated: The Qumran Texts in English*. Translated by Wilfred G. E. Watson. 2nd ed. Leiden: Brill, 1996.

Garland, David E. *A Theology of Mark's Gospel: Good News about Jesus the Messiah, the Son of God*. Biblical Theology of the New Testament. Grand Rapids: Zondervan, 2015.

———. *Mark*. The NIV Application Commentary. Grand Rapids: Zondervan, 1996.

Garrett, Susan R. *The Temptations of Jesus in Mark's Gospel*. Grand Rapids: Eerdmans, 1998.

Bibliography

Gathercole, Simon. *The Gospel and the Gospels: Christian Proclamation and Early Jesus Books*. Grand Rapids: Eerdmans, 2022.

Gerhardsson, Birger. *Memory and Manuscript: Oral Tradition and Written Transmission in Rabbinic Judaism and Early Christianity; with, Tradition & Transmission in Early Christianity*. The Biblical Resource Series. Grand Rapids: Eerdmans, 1998.

Gnilka, Joachim. *Jesus of Nazareth: Message and History*. Translated by Siegfried S. Schatzmann. Peabody, MA: Hendrickson, 1997.

Gombis, Timothy G. *Mark*. The Story of God Bible Commentary. Grand Rapids: Zondervan Academic, 2021.

Grant, Frederick C. *The Earliest Gospel: Studies of the Evangelic Tradition at Its Point of Crystallization in Writing*. Cole Lectures 1943. New York: Abingdon-Cokesbury, 1943.

———. "The Gospel According to St. Mark: Introduction and Exegesis." In *The Interpreter's Bible*, edited by George Arthur Buttrick et al., 7:627–917. 12 vols. New York: Abingdon-Cokesbury, 1951.

Guelich, Robert A. *Mark 1—8:26*. Word Biblical Commentary, 34A. Dallas: Word, 1989.

Guijarro, Santiago. *The Gospel of Mark in Context: A Social-Scientific Reading of the First Gospel*. Matrix: The Bible in Mediterranean Context 14. Eugene, OR: Cascade Books, 2022.

Gundry, Robert H. *Mark: A Commentary on His Apology for the Cross*. Grand Rapids: Eerdmans, 1993. Reprint in 2 vols. Grand Rapids: Eerdmans, 2004.

Hare, Douglas R. A. *Mark*. Westminster Bible Companion. Louisville: Westminster John Knox, 1996.

Harrington, Daniel J., SJ. *What Are They Saying About Mark?* 2nd ed. What Are They Saying About. New York: Paulist, 2005.

Harrington, Wilfred J., OP. *Reading Mark for the First Time*. New York: Paulist, 2013.

———. *What Was Mark At? The Gospel of Mark: A Commentary*. Blackrock, Ireland: Columba, 2008.

Hartman, Lars. *Mark for the Nations: A Text- and Reader-Oriented Commentary*. Eugene, OR: Pickwick Publications, 2010.

Hays, Richard B. *Echoes of Scripture in the Gospels*. Paperback ed. Waco, TX: Baylor University Press, 2017.

Healy, Mary. *The Gospel of Mark*. Catholic Commentary on Sacred Scripture. Grand Rapids: Baker Academic, 2008.

Hengel, Martin. *The Four Gospels and the One Gospel of Jesus Christ*. Harrisburg, PA: Trinity, 2000.

———. *Studies in the Gospel of Mark*. Philadelphia: Fortress, 1985.

Holmes, Michael W., ed. *The Greek New Testament: SBL Edition*. Atlanta: Society of Biblical Literature, 2010.

Hooker, Morna D. *The Gospel According to Saint Mark*. 1991. Reprint, Peabody, MA: Hendrickson, 1997.

Horsley, Richard A. *Galilee: History, Politics, People*. Valley Forge, PA: Trinity, 1995.

———. *Hearing the Whole Story: The Politics of Plot in Mark's Gospel*. Louisville: Westminster John Knox, 2001.

Horsley, Richard A., et al., eds. *Performing the Gospel: Orality, Memory, and Mark*. Minneapolis: Fortress, 2006.

Huck, Albert, and Heinrich Greeven. *Synopsis of the First Three Gospels: With the Addition of the Johannine Parallels*. 13th ed. Tübingen: Mohr Siebeck, 1981.

Hughes, Frank W. "The Gospel and Its Rhetoric in Galatians." In *Gospel in Paul: Studies on Corinthians, Galatians, and Romans for Richard N. Longenecker*, edited by L. Ann Jervis and Peter Richardson, 210–21. Journal for the Study of the New Testament Supplement Series 108. Sheffield: Sheffield Academic, 1994.

Hurtado, Larry W. *Mark*. Understanding the Bible Commentary Series. Grand Rapids: Baker, 2011.

Iersel, Bas M. F. van. *Mark: A Reader-Response Commentary*. Translated by W. H. Bisscheroux. Journal for the Study of the New Testament Supplement Series, 164. Sheffield: Sheffield Academic, 1998.

Iverson, Kelly R. *Reading Mark*. Cascade Companions. Eugene, OR: Cascade Books, 2023.

Jewett, Robert. *Romans: A Commentary*. Hermeneia. Minneapolis: Fortress, 2006.

Juel, Donald H. *The Gospel of Mark*. Interpreting Biblical Texts. Nashville: Abingdon, 1999.

Jülicher, Adolf. *Die Gleichnisreden Jesu*. 2 vols. in 1. 1910. Reprint, Darmstadt: Wissenschaftliche Buchgesellschaft, 1963

Kähler, Martin. *The So-Called Historical Jesus and the Historic, Biblical Christ*. Translated, edited, and with an introduction by Carl E. Braaten. Seminar Editions. Philadelphia: Fortress, 1964.

Kealy, Seán P., CSSp. *Mark's Gospel: A History of Its Interpretation; From the Beginning Until 1979*. New York: Paulist, 1982.

Kee, Howard Clark. *Community of the New Age: Studies in Mark's Gospel*. Philadelphia: Westminster, 1977.

Keener, Craig S. *Christobiography: Memory, History, and the Reliability of the Gospels*. Grand Rapids: Eerdmans, 2019.

Kelber, Werner H., ed. *The Passion in Mark: Studies on Mark 14–16*. Philadelphia: Fortress, 1976.

Keown, Mark J. *Jesus in a World of Colliding Empires: Mark's Jesus from the Perspective of Power and Expectations*. 2 vols. Eugene, OR: Wipf & Stock, 2018.

Kertelge, Karl. *Gemeinde und Amt im Neuen Testament*. Die Botschaft Gottes 2/32. Leipzig: St. Benno, 1975.

Kilgallen, John J., SJ. *A Brief Commentary on the Gospel of Mark*. New York: Paulist, 1989.

Kingsbury, Jack Dean. *The Christology of Mark's Gospel*. Philadelphia: Fortress, 1983.

———. *Conflict in Mark: Jesus, Authorities, Disciples*. Minneapolis: Fortress, 1989.

Kittredge, Cynthia Briggs. *A Lot of the Way Trees Were Walking: Poems from the Gospel of Mark*. Eugene, OR: Wipf & Stock, 2015.

Koester, Helmut. *Ancient Christian Gospels: Their History and Development*. Philadelphia: Trinity, 1990.

Lane, William L. *The Gospel of Mark: The English Text with Introduction, Exposition and Notes*. New International Commentary on the New Testament 2. Grand Rapids: Eerdmans, 1974.

Larsen, Matthew D. C. *Gospels Before the Book*. New York: Oxford University Press, 2018.

Le Donne, Anthony, gen. ed. *Christology in Mark's Gospel: 4 Views*. Critical Points. Grand Rapids: Zondervan Academic, 2021.

Le Peau, Andrew T. *Mark Through Old Testament Eyes: A Background and Application Commentary*. Through Old Testament Eyes. Grand Rapids: Kregel Academic, 2017.

Levine, Amy-Jill. *The Gospel of Mark: A Beginner's Guide to the Good News*. Nashville: Abingdon, 2023.

Lightfoot, R. H. *The Gospel Message of St. Mark*. 1950. Reprint, Oxford: Clarendon 1952.

Longstaff, Thomas R. W. "Crisis and Christology: The Theology of Mark's Gospel." *Perkins School of Theology Journal* 33 (1980) 28–40.
Loraux, Nicole. *The Invention of Athens: The Funeral Oration in the Classical City*. Translated by Alan Sheridan. Cambridge: Harvard University Press, 1986.
Malbon, Elizabeth Struthers. *Hearing Mark: A Listener's Guide*. Harrisburg, PA: Trinity, 2002.
———. *In the Company of Jesus: Characters in Mark's Gospel*. Louisville: Westminster John Knox, 2000.
———. *Mark's Jesus: Characterization as Narrative Christology*. Waco, TX: Baylor University Press, 2009.
———. *Narrative Space and Mythic Meaning in Mark*. San Francisco: Harper & Row, 1986.
Marcus, Joel. "The Jewish War and the *Sitz im Leben* of Mark." *Journal of Biblical Literature* 111 (1992) 441–62.
———. *Mark 1–8: A New Translation with Introduction and Commentary*. 2000. Reprint, Anchor Yale Bible 27. New Haven: Yale University Press, 2010.
———. *Mark 8–16: A New Translation with Introduction and Commentary*. Anchor Yale Bible 27A. New Haven: Yale University Press, 2009.
Martin, Ralph. *Mark: Evangelist and Theologian*. Contemporary Evangelical Perspectives. Grand Rapids: Zondervan, 1972.
Marxsen, Willi. *Mark the Evangelist: Studies on the Redaction History of the Gospel*. Translated by James Boyce and others. Nashville: Abingdon, 1969.
Matera, Frank J. *A Concise Theology of the New Testament*. Biblical Studies from the Catholic Biblical Association 1. Mahwah, NJ : Paulist, 2022.
Metts, Michael B. "Neglected Discontinuity Between Early Form Criticism and the New Quest with Reference to the Last Supper." In *Jesus, Skepticism, and the Problem of History: Criteria and Context in the Study of Christian Origins*, edited by Darrel L. Bock and J. Ed Komoszewski, 67–90. Grand Rapids: Zondervan Academic, 2019.
Meier, John P. *A Marginal Jew: Rethinking the Historical Jesus*. 5 vols. Anchor Bible Reference Library. Vols. 1–4, New York: Doubleday, 1991–2009. Vol. 5, New Haven: Yale University Press, 2016.
Migne, Jacques-Paul, ed. *Patrologiae Cursus Completus*: Series Latina 217 vols. Paris: Migne, 1844–1864.
Mitchell, Joan L. *Beyond Fear and Silence: A Feminist-Literary Reading of Mark*. New York: Continuum, 2001.
Moloney, Francis J., SDB. *The Gospel of Mark: A Commentary*. 2002. Repirnt, Grand Rapids: Baker Academic, 2012.
Mowinckel, Sigmund. *He That Cometh*. Translated by G. W. Anderson. New York: Abingdon, 1956.
Myers, Ched. *Binding the Strong Man: A Political Reading of Mark's Story of Jesus*. Maryknoll, NY: Orbis, 1988.
Neirynck, Frans, et al., comps. *The Gospel of Mark: A Cumulative Bibliography, 1950–1990*. Bibliotheca Ephemeridum Theologicarum Lovaniensium 102. Leuven: Leuven University Press and Peeters, 1992.
Nestle, Eberhard, and Erwin Nestle. *Novum Testamentum Graece*. Edited by Kurt Aland et al. 28th ed. Stuttgart: Deutsche Bibelgesellschaft, 2012.
———. *Novum Testamentum Graece*. Edited by Kurt Aland et al. 26th ed. Stuttgart: Deutsche Bibelstiftung, 1979.

Bibliography

Nineham, D. E. *Saint Mark.* 1963. Reprint, with minor revisions. Pelican New Testament Commentaries. Harmondsworth, UK: Penguin, 1969.

Orr, Peter. *The Beginning of the Gospel: A Theology of Mark.* New Testament Theology. Wheaton, IL: Crossway, 2023.

Painter, John. *Mark's Gospel.* New Testament Readings. London: Routledge, 1997.

Perez i Diaz, Mar. *Mark, a Pauline Theologian: A Re-reading of the Traditions of Jesus in the Light of Paul's Theology.* Wissenschaftliche Untersuchungen zum Neuen Testament, 2/521. Tübingen: Mohr Siebeck, 2020.

Perkins, Pheme. *The Gospel of Mark: Introduction, Commentary, and Reflections.* In *The New Interpreter's Bible,* edited by Leander E. Keck et al., 8:507–733. 12 vols. Nashville: Abingdon, 1994.

———. *Introduction to the Synoptic Gospels.* Grand Rapids: Eerdmans, 2007.

Pervo, Richard I. *Profit with Delight: The Literary Genre of the Acts of the Apostles.* Philadelphia: Fortress, 1987.

Peterson, Dwight N. *The Origins of Mark: The Markan Community in Current Debate.* Biblical Interpretation Series 48. Leiden: Brill, 2000.

Placher, William C. *Mark.* Belief: A Theological Commentary on the Bible. Louisville: Westminster John Knox, 2010.

Reese, James M., OSFS. *The Student's Guide to the Gospels.* Good News Studies 24. Collegeville, MN: Liturgical, 1992.

Rhoads, David, et al. *Mark as Story: An Introduction to the Narrative of a Gospel.* 2nd ed. Minneapolis: Fortress, 1999.

Robbins, Vernon K. *Jesus the Teacher: A Socio-Rhetorical Interpretation of Mark.* 1984. Reprint, with a new interoduction. Paperback ed. Minneapolis: Fortress, 1992.

Robinson, James M. *The Gospel of Jesus: In Search of the Original Good News.* San Francisco: HarperSanFrancisco, 2005.

———. *The Problem of History in Mark and Other Marcan Studies.* Philadelphia: Fortress, 1982.

Roskam, H. N. *The Purpose of the Gospel of Mark in Its Historical and Social Context.* Supplements to Novum Testamentum, 114. Leiden: Brill, 2004.

Roth, Wolfgang. *Hebrew Gospel: Cracking the Code of Mark.* 1988. Reprint, Eugene, OR: Wipf & Stock, 2009.

Sabin, Marie Noonan. *The Gospel According to Mark.* New Collegeville Bible Commentary. New Testament 2. Collegeville, MN: Liturgical, 2006.

———. *Reopening the Word: Reading Mark as Theology in the Context of Early Judaism.* Oxford: Oxford University Press, 2002.

Schmidt, Daryl D. *The Gospel of Mark, with Introduction, Notes, and Original Text.* The Scholars Bible 1. Salem, OR: Polebridge, 1990.

Schmidt, Karl Ludwig. *The Framework of the Story of Jesus: Literary-Critical Investigations of the Earliest Jesus Tradition.* Translated by Byron R. McCane. Eugene, OR: Cascade Books, 2021.

Schnabel, Eckhard J. *Mark: An Introduction and Commentary.* 2nd ed. Tyndale New Testament Commentaries 2. Downers Grove, IL: IVP Academic, 2017.

Schnackenburg, Rudolf. *The Gospel According to St. Mark.* Translated by Werner Kruppa. 2 vols. New Testament for Spiritual Reading 3–4. 1971. Reprint, New York: Crossroad, 1981.

Schulz, Siegfried. "Mark's Significance for the Theology of Early Christianity." In *The Interpretation of Mark*, edited by W. R. Telford, 197–206. 2nd ed. Studies in New Testament Interpretation. Edinburgh: T. & T. Clark, 1995.

Schweitzer, Albert. *The Quest of the Historical Jesus: First Complete Edition*. Edited by John Bowden. Minneapolis: Fortress, 2001.

Schweizer, Eduard. *The Good News According to Mark*. Translated by Donald H. Madvig. Richmnd, VA: John Knox, 1970.

Shiner, Whitney Taylor. *Follow Me! Disciples in Markan Rhetoric*. Society of Biblical Literature Dissertation Series 145. Atlanta: Scholars, 1995.

———. *Proclaiming the Gospel: First-Century Performance of Mark*. Harrisburg, PA: Trinity, 2003.

Smith, Abraham. *Mark: An Introduction and Study Guide; Shaping the Life and Legacy of Jesus*. T & T Clark Study Guides to the New Testament 2. London: Bloomsbury T. & T. Clark, 2017.

Spencer, F. Scott. *Reading Mark: A Literary and Theological Commentary*. Reading the New Testament, 2nd series. Macon, GA: Smith & Helwys, 2023.

Stegemann, Hartmut. *The Library of Qumran: On the Essenes, Qumran, John the Baptist, and Jesus*. Grand Rapids: Eerdmans, 1998.

Stein, Robert H. *Mark*. Baker Exegetical Commentary on the New Testament. Grand Rapids: Baker Academic, 2008.

Stewart, Alistair. *The Original Bishops: Office and Order in the First Christian Communities*. Grand Rapids: Baker Academic, 2014.

Strack, Hermann L., and Paul Billerbeck. *A Commentary on the New Testament from the Talmud & Midrash*. Edited by Jacob N. Cerone et al. Translated by Andrew Bowden and Joseph Longarino. With an introduction by David Instone-Brewer. 3 vols. Bellingham, WA: Lexham, 2022.

Strauss, Mark L. *Mark*. Zondervan Exegetical Commentary on the New Testament. Grand Rapids: Zondervan Academic, 2014.

Strecker, Georg. *Theology of the New Testament*. German ed. edited and completed by Friedrich Wilhelm Horn. Translated by M. Eugene Boring. New York: de Gruyter, 2000.

Streeter, Burnett Hillman. *The Four Gospels: A Study of Origins*. 4th impression, revised. London: Macmillans, 1930.

Strutwolf, Holger, et al., eds. *The Greek New Testament*. 5th rev. ed. Stuttgart: Deutsche Bibelgesellschaft, 2014.

Strutwolf, Holger, et al., eds. *Novum Testamentum Graece*. 28th rev. ed. Stuttgart: Deutsche Bibelgesellschaft, 2012.

Strutwolf, Holger, et al., eds. *Novum Testamentum Graecum: editio critica maior*. Vol. 1.2/1, *The Gospel According to Mark: The Text*. Stuttgart: Deutsche Bibelgesellschaft, 2021.

Sweat, Laura C. *The Theological Role of Paradox in the Gospel of Mark: Profiles from the History of Interpretation*. T. & T. Clark Library of Biblical Studies. Library of New Testament Studies 492. London: Bloomsbury T & T Clark, 2013.

Swete, Henry Barclay. *The Gospel According to St. Mark: The Greek Text with Introduction, Notes, and Indices*. 3rd ed. London: Macmillan, 1913.

Tan, Kim Huat. *Mark*. New Covenant Commentary Series. Eugene, OR: Cascade Books, 2015.

Taylor, Vincent. *The Formation of the Gospel Tradition*, 2nd ed. London: Macmillan, 1933.

———. *The Gospel According to St. Mark: The Greek Text with Introduction, Notes, and Indexes.* 2nd ed. New York: St. Martin's, 1966.
Telford, W. R., ed. *The Interpretation of Mark.* 2nd ed. Studies in New Testament Interpretation. Edinburgh: T. & T. Clark, 1995.
———. *The Theology of the Gospel of Mark.* New Testament Theology. Cambridge: Cambridge University Press, 1999.
———. *Writing on the Gospel of Mark.* Guides to Advanced Biblical Research 1. Blandford Forum, UK: Deo, 2009.
Theissen, Gerd. *The Gospels in Context: Social and Political History in the Synoptic Tradition.* Translated by Linda M. Maloney. Minneapolis: Fortress, 1991.
Thompson, Mary R., SSMN. *The Role of Disbelief in Mark: A New Approach to the Second Gospel.* New York: Paulist, 1989.
Tischendorf, Constantin von. *Novum Testamentum Graece Ad Antiquissimos Testes Denuo Recensuit, Apparatum Criticum Omni Studio Perfectum,* editio octava critica maior. 1869. Reprint, London: Forgotten Books, 2018.
Tolbert, Mary Ann. *Sowing the Gospel: Mark's World in Literary-Historical Perspective.* Minneapolis: Fortress, 1989.
Trocmé, Etienne. *The Formation of the Gospel According to Mark.* Translated by Pamela Gaughan. Philadelphia: Westminster, 1975.
Tuckett, Christopher, ed. *The Messianic Secret.* Issues in Religion and Theology 1. Philadelphia: Fortress, 1983.
Tyndale House (Library). *The Greek New Testament.* Produced at Tyndale House, Cambridge. Edited by Dirk Jongkind et al. Wheaton, IL: Crossway, 2017.
University of Navarre Faculty of Theology. *Saint Mark's Gospel in the Revised Standard Version and New Vulgate.* With a Commentary by Members of the Faculty of Theology at the University of Navarre. 2nd ed. The Navarre Bible. Blackrock, Ireland: Four Courts, 1992.
Van Linden, Philip, CM. *The Gospel According to Mark.* Collegeville Bible Commentary 2. Collegeville, MN: Liturgical, 1983.
Vermes, Géza. *The Authentic Gospel of Jesus.* London: Penguin, 2004.
———. *Jesus and the World of Judaism.* Philadelphia: Fortress, 1984.
———. *Jesus in His Jewish Context.* Minneapolis: Fortress, 2003.
———. *Jesus the Jew: A Historian's Reading of the Gospels.* Philadelphia: Fortress, 1975.
Vernant, J.-P. *Problèms de la guerre en Grèce ancienne.* Civilisations et sociétés 11. Paris: Mouton, 1968.
Voelz, James W. *Mark 1:1—8:26.* Concordia Commentaries. St. Louis: Concordia, 2013.
Voelz, James W., and Christopher W. Mitchell. *Mark 8:27—16:20.* Concordia Commentaries. St. Louis: Concordia, 2019.
Vorster, Willem S. "The Function of the Use of the Old Testament in Mark." *Neotestamentica* 14 (1981) 62–72.
Watson, Francis. *The Fourfold Gospel: A Theological Reading of the New Testament Portraits of Jesus.* Grand Rapids: Baker Academic, 2016.
Watts, Rikki E. *Isaiah's New Exodus in Mark.* 1997. Reprint, Grand Rapids: Baker, 2000.
Weeden, Theodore J. *Mark—Traditions in Conflict.* Philadelphia: Fortress, 1971.
Winn, Adam. *Mark and the Elijah-Elisha Narrative: Considering the Practice of Greco-Roman Imitation in the Search for Markan Source Material.* Eugene, OR: Pickwick Publications, 2010.

———. *The Purpose of Mark's Gospel: An Early Christian Response to Roman Imperial Propaganda.* Wissenschaftliche Untersuchungen zum Neuen Testament 2/245. Tübingen: Mohr Siebeck, 2008.

Wischmeyer, Oda, et al., eds. *Paul and Mark: Comparative Essays Part I; Two Authors at the Beginnings of Christianity.* Beihefte zur Zeitschrift für die neutestamentliche Wissenschaft 198. Berlin: de Gruyter, 2014.

Witherington, Ben, III. *The Gospel of Mark: A Socio-Rhetorical Commentary.* Grand Rapids: Eerdmans, 2001.

Wrede, William. *The Messianic Secret.* Translated by J. C. G. Grieg. Library of Theological Translations. Greenwood, SC: Attic, 1971.

Young, Brad H. *Jesus the Jewish Theologian.* Peabody, MA: Hendrickson, 1995.

Zanchettin, Leo, ed. *Mark: A Devotional Commentary. Meditations on the Gospel According to St. Mark.* Frederick, MD: The Word Among Us, 1998.

Index of Scripture and Other Ancient Literature

HEBREW BIBLE

Genesis

1:1—2:4a	78
2:4b—3:24	78
2:24	78

Exodus

3:4–6	95
3:6	95
20:8–10	34

Leviticus

19:18	2, 96

Deuteronomy

5:12–15	34
6:4–5	96
6:5	2
24:1–4	78

1 Samuel

21:1–6	34

1 Kings

1 Kgs 17—2 Kgs 13	15, 16, 67

2 Kings

1:8	19, 19n6
2:9	64

Psalms

22:2	110
110	97
110:1	97
118:22–23	93

Isaiah

5:1–7	89, 92
5:5–6	89
40:3	17, 18, 19, 20, 54, 67

Daniel

9:27	100
11:31	100
12:11	100

Amos

2:4–5	59n1
2:6–11	59n1
7:10–17	59n1

Zechariah

9:9	87
9:10, 16	87

Malachi

3:1	17, 18, 19, 20, 67

NEW TESTAMENT

Matthew

2:1–23	29
3:14–15	21
3:24–30	44
6:10	77
8:27	49n4
8:28–34	48
13:13–17	20
14:13–21	55n5
15:28	62
16:13–33	69
16:17–19	76
16:18	77
16:24	72
17:22–23	69
19:1–9	78
19:3–12	79
19:30	33
20:16	33
20:17–28	69
21:1–9	109
21:33–46	92
22:23–33	9
24	122
25:35–40	77n4
26:6–13	103
26:26–39	7n6
27:3–9	103
27:6	104
27:10	104
28:1–8	115
28:8	115

Mark

1:1—16:8	66, 74
1:1—8:26	3, 67
1:1–15	14–23, 17, 22
1:1	21n8, 22, 115
1:2–11	17
1:2–6	54
1:2–3	17, 19, 20
1:2	17, 67
1:3–4	20
1:3	18, 67, 68
1:5	19
1:6	19n6
1:7–8	20
1:7	19
1:9–11	18, 20, 21, 69
1:9	46n2
1:10	21, 31
1:11	20, 31, 38, 67, 68, 73, 124
1:12–13	20, 22, 68
1:12	21, 68
1:14–15	22, 68
1:14	21, 21n8, 22
1:15	21n8, 22, 67
1:16—3:6	24–36
1:16–18	24
1:17	25
1:19–20	24, 84
1:21–28	35
1:21	25
1:23–28	26, 31
1:27–28	35
1:27	25
1:28	35
1:29–31	30
1:32–34	30, 36
1:34	30
1:35–39	30
1:36	17
1:40–45	31, 36
1:40–41	31
1:43–44	31
1:45—2:2	36
1:45	31, 36
2:1–12	31, 34
2:1	31
2:5–9	31, 34
2:10	31
2:13–17	31–32
2:15	32
2:16	32
2:17	32
2:18–22	33
2:21–22	33

Index of Scripture and Other Ancient Literature

2:23–28	34	4:39	47
3:1–6	34–36	4:41	47
3:1–2	35, 36	5:1–20	46, 48–49, 53, 58, 63
3:2	35	5:1	46, 49
3:3–4	35	5:2–5	49
3:3	35	5:3–5	48
3:4–5a	35	5:6–12	49
3:5b	35	5:9	48
3:6	35, 36	5:11–13	49
3:7—4:34	37–45	5:13	49
3:7–12	37–38	5:14–17	49
3:7–10	37	5:15	49
3:9–10	37	5:17–18	49
3:9	41	5:17	49
3:11	37	5:18–19	49
3:12	37	5:20	49
3:13–19	38–39, 38n1	5:21–43	50–51
3:14	39, 39n4	5:22–24	50
3:19	24	5:25–27	50
3:20–21	39–40	5:28	50
3:21	40	5:29	50
3:22	40	5:30	50
3:22–30	40	5:34	50
3:26	40	5:35	50
3:31–35	40–41	5:36	50
3:31	40	5:39	50
3:35	40	5:41	50
4:1–41	120	5:43	50
4:1–9	41, 43	6:1–6a	46, 51–53
4:1–2	41	6:2–3	52
4:2	41	6:3	52
4:3–10	41	6:5	53
4:10–20	41–43	6:6a	53
4:11	43	6:6b–13	46, 53
4:19	42	6:14–29	74
4:21–32	43–44	6:14–16	53–54
4:21–25	43	6:15	53
4:21–22	43	6:16	54
4:23	43	6:17–29	21, 46, 54–55
4:26–29	44	6:30–31	55
4:28	44	6:30	39n4
4:30–32	44	6:32–44	55–57, 65
4:33–34	44–45	6:32–40	55n5
4:34	10, 13, 43, 47	6:32–34	55
4:35—6:56	46–58	6:34	56
4:35–41	46–48, 53	6:35–38	56
4:35–36	47	6:39–41	56
4:38	47	6:42–44	56

143

Mark (continued)

6:44	56
6:45–52	46, 57–58
6:45	58
6:47	57
6:49	57
6:51	57
6:52	58
6:53–56	46, 58
6:56	58
7:1—8:26	59–61
7:1–23	59–61
7:1–16	61
7:1	60
7:2	60
7:3–4	60
7:5	60
7:16	60, 60n3
7:17–23	60, 61
7:17	61
7:19	61
7:21–22	61
7:24–30	61–63
7:25	62
7:27–28	62
7:29	62
7:31–37	63, 64, 66
7:31	63
7:35	64
7:37	64, 65, 120
8:1–38	47
8:10	65
8:1–10	64–65
8:11–13	65
8:12	65
8:13	65
8:14–21	65–66
8:15	65
8:16	65
8:22–26	66
8:25	66
8:26	66, 67
8:27—16:8	3, 67
8:27—10:52	69
8:27–33	122
8:27–30	3, 30, 31, 59, 69–70
8:27–28	70
8:27	69, 73
8:28–29	53
8:29	23, 47, 67
8:30	70
8:31–34	69
8:31–33	59, 70–72
8:31	71, 122
8:32–33	83
8:33	122
8:34—9:1	72
8:34	71, 72
8:35	21n8
8:38	72
9:1	72
9:2–13	73–75
9:2–10	74
9:2–8	75
9:7	73
9:9–11	19n6
9:9	73
9:10	73
9:11–13	74
9:11	74
9:12	74
9:14–29	75–76
9:14–15	75
9:19–24	75
9:22	76
9:23	76
9:24	76
9:25	75
9:26	75
9:27	75
9:30–37	69, 122
9:30–32	76
9:31	73, 76, 122
9:32	76
9:33–37	76–77
9:35	82
9:38–41	77
9:42–50	77–78
10:1–12	78–79
10:2–12	79
10:2	78
10:5	78
10:9	78
10:10–12	79
10:10	78

Reference	Page	Reference	Page
10:13–16	80	12:7	93
10:13	80	12:9	93
10:14	80	12:10–12	93
10:15	80	12:12	93
10:17–31	82	12:13–17	94
10:17–22	80–81	12:13	94
10:17	80, 81	12:17	94
10:18	80	12:18–27	9, 94–95
10:19	80	12:23	95
10:20	80	12:26–27	95
10:21	81	12:26	95
10:22	81	12:27	95
10:23–31	81–83	12:28–34	96–97
10:25	82–83	12:28	96, 97
10:29	21n8	12:29–30	96
10:31	33, 82	12:31	96
10:32–34	69, 83–84, 122	12:32–33	96
10:32	82	12:34	96
10:34	122	12:35–37	97
10:35–45	84	12:36	97
10:37	84	12:37b–40	97–98
10:45	71	12:37b	97
10:46–52	84–85	12:40	97–98
10:47–48	85	12:41–44	98
10:49	85	12:41	98
10:52	85	12:43	98
11:1—13:37	86–101	13:1–2	98–99
11:1–11	89	13:2	98
11:1–10	65, 70, 86–89, 109	13:3–13	99–100
11:1b–6	104	13:4–27	122
11:2–6	87	13:4	99
11:7–10	87	13:8	99
11:11	88	13:9–13	99
11:12–14	89, 100	13:9	99
11:12	89	13:10	21n8, 99
11:14	89	13:13	100
11:15–17	88–90	13:14–20	100
11:18–19	90–91	13:21–23	100
11:18	90	13:21–22	100
11:20–26	89	13:24–27	99, 100
11:20–21	100	13:24–25	100
11:27–33	91–92, 94	13:26–27	100
11:27–32	93	13:28–32	100–101
11:27	91	13:28	101
11:30	91	13:31	101
11:31	91	13:32	101
12:1–12	92–93	13:33–37	101
12:6	93	13:35–37	101

Mark (continued)

13:37	101
14:1—15:47	26, 74, 102–113
14:1-2	102–103, 108
14:2	106
14:3-9	103
14:4	103
14:5	103
14:8	103
14:9	21n8, 103
14:10-11	103–104
14:10	24
14:11	104
14:12-17	104
14:18-21	104
14:19	104
14:22-25	7n6, 104–105
14:25	105
14:26-31	105–106
14:29	105
14:30	10, 105, 107
14:31	105
14:31b	106
14:32-42	106
14:35-36	106
14:35	106
14:43-52	106–7
14:43	24, 106
14:44	106
14:48-49	106
14:50	106
14:51-52	107
14:53-65	107, 108
14:53	107
14:54	107
14:61-62	107
14:63-65	107
14:66-72	107
14:68	107
14:70	107
14:71	107
14:72	10, 107
15:1-5	108
15:1	109
15:2-5	109
15:2	108
15:5	108
15:6-47	21
15:6-14	108–109
15:6	108
15:13-14	109
15:14	109
15:16-20a	109
15:20b-21	110
15:22-26	110
15:22	110
15:23	110
15:25	110
15:26	110
15:27-32b	110
15:29-32	110
15:33-39	110–111
15:33	110
15:34	110
15:35	110
15:36	110
15:38	110
15:39	110–111
15:40-41	111
15:42-47	111–113
15:44-45	111
15:46	111
15:47	111, 114
16:1-8	11, 13, 52, 52, 64, 65, 74, 102, 107, 114–117, 120, 122, 126
16:3-4	115
16:5-8	58
16:6	115
16:7	117
16:8	74, 117, 123, 125, 127
16:9-20	67, 114, 116–117
16:15	21n8

Luke

1:1—2:52	29
3:21-22	20, 21
7:36-50	103
8:26-39	48
9:10b-17	55n5
9:18-22	69
9:23	72
9:43-48	69
10:1-12	38
10:17-20	38

Index of Scripture and Other Ancient Literature

11:2	77
13:30	33
18:31–34	69
19:28–40	109
20:9–19	92
20:27–40	9
21	122
22:15–20	7n6
24:1–12	115
24:9	115
24:50–53	116

John

6:1–15	55n5
12:1–8	103
12:12–16	109
13:1–20	7n7
19:26	111
20:24–28	123

Acts

1:6–11	116
1:21–22	39, 73

Romans

16:1–2	39
16:7	39

1 Corinthians

3:5	39
9:18	8n8
11:23–26	7n6, 104
12	124
15:1	8n8
15:3–11	4
15:3–8	122
15:3–4	71
15:8	5
15:12–19	71

2 Corinthians

5:21	21n7
10:1—13:13	12

Galatians

3:28	62

1 Thessalonians

4:13—5:3	122

2 Thessalonians

1:7–10, 2:8	122

Titus

2:11–13	122

Hebrews

4:15	21n7

1 Peter

1:3–6	122

Revelation

1:4–5	122
1:7–8	122

OTHER ANCIENT LITERATURE

Augustine

De consensu evangelistarum	6
Harmony of the Gospels	6

1 Clement

	4

Dead Sea Scrolls

1QM (War Scroll)	18
11QTemple	38n1

Epistle of Barnabas

6:13	82

Eusebius

Ecclesiastical History 3.39.15	105n4

Freer Logion

	116–17

Gregory the Great

Moralia 4	VII

Jerome

Commentary on Isaiah	VII

Oxyrhynchus Papyri

654, 21–27	82

Index of Authors

Achtemeier, Paul J., 30n6, 131
Aland, Barbara, 131
Aland, Kurt, 6n5, 82n8, 84n9, 131
Allison, Dale C., 104n3, 131

Beavis, Mary Ann, VIII, 131
Becker, Eve-Marie, 124n4, 131
Bernier, Jonathan, 28n5, 131
Best, Ernest, 131
Billerbeck, Paul, 94n3, 138
Black, C. Clifton, VIII, 123n3, 131
Bock, Darrell, 132
Borg, Marcus J., 132
Boring, M. Eugene, VIII, 132
Bornkamm, Günther, 132
Branscomb, B. Harvie, 132
Bryan, Christopher, 132
Bultmann, Rudolf, 25, 26n2, 26n3, 28n4, 45, 118, 132
Burkill, T. A., 132
Burridge, Richard A., 132
Byrne, Brendan, S.J., 23n9, 132

Carroll, John T., 132
Carter, Warren, 132
Chilton, Bruce, 132
Cole, R. Alan, 132
Collins, John J., 132
Collins, Raymond F., IX, 132
Cranfield, C. E. B., 132
Crawford, Barry S., 132
Culpepper, R. Alan, 132

Davies, W. D., 104n3, 133
Dewey, Joanna, 133

Dibelius, Martin, 26n3, 45, 133
Donahue, John R., S.J., 133
Driggers, Ira Brent, 133
Dunn, James D. G., 133
Dykstra, Tom, 133

Easton, Burton Scott, 133
Edwards, James R., 133
Eichrodt, Walther, 61n4, 133
Elliott, J. K., 133
Evans, Craig A., 133
Focant, Camille, 133
Francis, Pope, 133
Freyne, Sean, 104n2, 133

García Martínez, Florentino, 18n4, 133
Garland, David E., VIII, 23n9, 123n3, 126–127, 133
Garrett, Susan R., 133
Gathercole, Simon, 134
Gerhardsson, Birger, 134
Gnilka, Joachim, 17n2, 71, 87–88, 99n4, 109n5, 112, 134
Gombis, Timothy G., 134
Grant, Frederick C., 123n3, 134
Greeven, Heinrich, 39n5, 134
Guelich, Robert A., 134
Guijarro, Santiago, 134
Gundry, Robert H., 134

Hare, Douglas R. A., 134
Harrington, Daniel J., S.J., 134
Harrington, Wilfred J., O.P., 134
Hartman, Lars, 134
Hays, Richard B., 134

Index of Authors

Healy, Mary, 134
Hengel, Martin, 134
Holmes, Michael W., 39n5, 134
Hooker, Morna D., 134
Horsley, Richard A., 99n4, 134
Huck, Albert, 39n5, 134
Hughes, Frank W., 8n8, 135
Hurtado, Larry W., 135

Iersel, Bas M. F. van, 135, 139
Iverson, Kelly R., 135

Jewett, Robert, 32n7, 135
Juel, Donald H., 135
Jülicher, Adolf, 41n6, 135

Kähler, Martin, 102, 135
Kealy, Seán P., C.S.Sp., 135
Kee, Howard Clark, 135
Keener, Craig S., 26n3, 135
Kelber, Werner H., 135
Keown, Mark J., 135
Kertelge, Karl, 38n3, 135
Kilgallen, John J., S.J., 135
Kingsbury, Jack Dean, 24n1, 135
Kittredge, Cynthia Briggs, 135
Koester, Helmut, 135

Lane, William L., 135
Larsen, Matthew D. C., 135
Le Donne, Anthony, 135
Le Peau, Andrew T., 135
Levine, Amy-Jill, 135
Lightfoot, R. H., 135
Longstaff, Thomas R. W., 136
Loraux, Nicole, 33n8, 136

Malbon, Elizabeth Struthers, 136
Marcus, Joel, 35n9, 100n5, 136
Martin, Ralph, 136
Marxsen, Willi, 136
Matera, Frank J., 123n3, 136
Meier, John P., 136
Metts, Michael B., 27n3, 136
Mitchell, Joan L., 136
Moloney, Francis J., S.D.B., 23n9, 136
Mowinckel, Sigmund, 70n1, 136
Myers, Ched, 136

Neirynck, Frans, 136
Nineham, D. E., 137

Orr, Peter, 137

Painter, John, 137
Perez i Diaz, Mar, 137
Perkins, Pheme, VIII, 137
Pervo, Richard I., VIII, 48, 137
Petersen, Dwight N., 137
Placher, William C., 137

Reese, James M., O.S.F.S., 137
Rhodes, David, 137
Robbins, Vernon K., 137
Robinson, James M., 137
Roskam, H. N., 137
Roth, Wolfgang, VIII, 15n1, 16, 19n6, 64, 120, 137

Sabin, Marie Noonan, 137
Schmidt, Daryl D., 137
Schmidt, Karl Ludwig, 25, 137
Schnabel, Eckhard J., 137
Schnackenburg, Rudolf, 137
Schulz, Siegfried, 123n3, 138
Schweitzer, Albert, 3, 13, 138
Schweizer, Eduard, 138
Shiner, Whitney Taylor, 138
Smith, Abraham, 138
Spencer, F. Scott, 138
Stegemann, Hartmut, 18n5, 138
Stein, Robert H., 138
Stewart, Alastair, 38n3, 138
Strack, Hermann L., 94n3, 138
Strauss, Mark L., 138
Strecker, Georg, 123n3, 138
Streeter, Burnett Hillman, 6, 138
Strutwolf, Holger, 138
Sweat, Laura C., 138
Swete, Henry Barclay, VIII, 138

Tan, Kim Huat, 138
Taylor, Vincent, VIII, 66, 82n7, 90n2, 123n3, 138
Telford, William R., 123n3, 125–127, 139
Theissen, Gerd, 139
Thompson, Mary R., S.S.M.N., 139

Index of Authors

Tischendorf, Constantin von, 60n3, 139
Tolbert, Mary Ann, 139
Trocmé, Etienne, 139
Tuckett, Christopher, 139

Van Linden, Philip, C.M., 139
Vermes, Géza, 60n2, 104n2, 139
Vernant, J.-P., 33n8, 139
Voelz, James W., 139
Vorster, Willem S., 139

Watson, Francis, 139
Watts, Rikki E., 139
Weeden, Theodore J., 139
Winn, Adam, 139–140
Wischmeyer, Oda, 124n4, 140
Witherington, Ben, III, 140
Wrede, William, 140

Yarbro Collins, Adela, VIII, 38n1, 140
Young, Brad H., 140

Zanchettin, Leo, 140

www.ingramcontent.com/pod-product-compliance
Lightning Source LLC
Chambersburg PA
CBHW022122160426
43197CB00009B/1121